English I Miss

(Friendly activities addressing errors
English language learners make)

Connie Turner
and
Judy Shane

Dominie Press, Inc.

Publisher: Raymond Yuen
Executive Editor: Carlos A. Byfield
Editor: Bob Rowland
Designer: Carol Anne Craft

Published by:

 **Dominie Press, Inc.**

1949 Kellogg Avenue
Carlsbad, California 92008 USA

ISBN 0-7685-0462-7
Printed in Singapore by PH Productions Pte. Ltd.
1 2 3 4 5 6 PH 01 00 99

Table of Contents

Table of Contents

English I Missed began in the classroom. The goal was to provide standard English in short, clear, friendly activities that address common errors students make—especially students who are **LEP;** **at risk;** in **middle, high,** and **adult schools, special education,** and **alternative education** programs such as **independent study, home study, continuation, GAIN, juvenile court,** and **community schools.**

As the title promises, *English I Missed* targets specific misuse that has endured in spite of instruction. You'll discover other differences from the standard language book: we use **phraseology** that our research shows students respond to, the first practice for students is in **story** form, and **lessons are designed around student errors.**

This book can be used in a number of ways. Here are three:

1. **Whole class.** Pair/group activities such as students generating their own sentences, checking each other's answers, giving dictation, or playing a "What's Wrong With This Sentence" game follow a teacher-directed lesson.

2. **Clinics.** Students are grouped by errors they make on the pre/post test. A short directed lesson is followed by activities listed above.

3. **One-on-One.** Teacher matches student writing error (for example, misuse of *stayed* and *stood*) with corresponding page from <u>*English I Missed,*</u> teaches it, and then has student practice and correct his or her own writing.

Throughout the book, you will find references to *standard* English. We view standard English as the language of advancement in academic, business, and other formal settings. Whether standard English is a first or second language, command of this language is a major determinant of success.

We hope you find these materials helpful and that your students enjoy learning from them. We welcome any comments at IZZYGATO@aol.com.

Sincerely,
Connie Turner and Judy Shane

Accept

Use **accept** when you agree to take something that someone gives you.

Example:
Thank you so much! I **accept** the Oscar!

Except

Use **except** when something or someone is left out.

Example:
Everyone won **except** my favorite actor.

Practice: Write **accept** or **except** in the spaces below.

My friends say I could be an actor _____ for one thing.
₁

I am very shy. It is even hard for me to _____ compliments
₂

(_____ from my girlfriend). She says that I have talent.
₃

I say, "I _____ that." She says that I am good-looking.
₄

I _____ that. She says everything I want _____
₅   ₆

"You deserve an Oscar."

Write **accept** or **except** in the spaces below. Use **accept** to talk about what you'll take; use **except** to show what is left out.

1. Please _____ my invitation.

2. He won't _____ any money.

3. We're open every day _____ Monday.

4. The whole class was invited _____ for me.

5. The dog won't _____ her puppies.

6. Do you _____ checks?

7. I want everything on my hamburger _____ onions.

8. Please _____ my apology.

9. I like everyone _____ her.

10. I did all my homework _____ for one question.

11. She said she would _____ me as I am, and then she tried to change me!

Now write your own sentences using **accept** and **except**.

1. _____

2. _____

Don't use **ain't** or **ain't got.**

Why not? It's not standard English.

Use		Examples:	
am not		*Examples:*	I <u>am not</u> very lucky.
aren't			There <u>aren't</u> any jobs.
isn't			This <u>isn't</u> my day.
doesn't have			He <u>doesn't have</u> a problem.
don't have			We <u>don't have</u> milk.
haven't			They <u>haven't</u> gone.

Practice: Write **am not**, **aren't**, **isn't**, **doesn't have**, **don't have**, or **haven't** in the spaces below.

I _____ any money. My girlfriend _____ any
    1   2

money. There _____ any jobs. Anyway, they all want a
              3

high-school diploma. I guess I _____ going out tonight.
                                4

It _____ fair. I could ask my sister to lend me some
   5

bread, but I _____ paid her back from last time.
              6

Nothing works out for me. I just _____ lucky.
                                  7

Write **am not**, **aren't**, **isn't**, **doesn't have**, **don't have**, or **haven't** in the spaces below. Remember, *ain't* isn't standard English.

1. I _____ going home.

2. He _____ going to give it to me.

3. They _____ my friends.

4. We _____ eating there.

5. She _____ his girlfriend.

6. They _____ a car.

7. He said, "It _____ right," and I agree.

8. He _____ his little brother with him.

9. I _____ time, and he _____ money.

10. They _____ idiots, and I _____ going to be a part of it.

11. _____ this Jennie's sweatshirt?

Now write your own sentence using **am not** instead of **ain't**.

1. _____

Anywhere

Use **anywhere** when you mean at any place.

Example:
My keys could be **anywhere.**

Everywhere

Use **everywhere** when you mean in all places.

Example:
I have looked **everywhere** for my keys.

Practice: Write **anywhere** or **everywhere** in the spaces below.

At night in the desert, the stars are _____.
1

_____ I look, I see hundreds of them. Millions.
2

There must be a place without a star! But I look and I look, and there are

stars _____. I do not see a starless place _____.
3   4

Somewhere, is there a sky without any stars? Or, is there a star

_____ without a sky?
5

Anywhere and Everywhere • Practice

Write **anywhere** or **everywhere** in the spaces below. Remember, **anywhere** refers to one place; **everywhere** refers to all places.

1. _____ I go, I see you!

2. I never go _____ without my pager.

3. I can't take you _____ today.

4. I can't always take you _____ you want to go.

5. Is there _____ you haven't been?

6. I've looked _____ for my bag.

7. I want to go _____ I want.

8. The smoke was _____.

9. Are you going _____ in particular?

10. She's going _____ she has always wanted to go.

Now write your own sentences using **anywhere** and **everywhere**.

1. _____

2. _____

Ask

Use **ask** when there's a question in your statement.

Example:
I was going to **ask** you if you could come over.

Tell

Use **tell** when you are making a statement.

Example:
I was going to **tell** you to come over.

Practice: Write **ask** or **tell** in the spaces below.

I will _____ my mom I want to drop out of school. She will
₁

cry, but I'll _____ her that I can get my G.E.D. Everything will
₂

be cool. I will _____ my counselor that I have her permission.
₃

He will _____ me if I am sure that I want to drop out. Then he
₄

will _____ my mother she has to come to school to sign me out.
₅

_____ me if I think this will work.
₆

Write **ask** or **tell** in the spaces below. Use **tell** only when your sentence is a statement; use **ask** when you don't know the answer, or need permission.

1. I am going to _____ her if she will marry me.

2. They want to _____ you if they can borrow some money.

3. We need to _____ if you can get there by bus.

4. She is so bossy! She always wants to _____ me what to do.

5. _____ me my times tables.

6. Did you _____ him if you could come over?

7. _____ me how old you are.

8. I was going to _____ you if I could come to see you now.

9. I want to _____ you if I passed.

10. I want to _____ you that you passed with flying colors.

11. I want to _____ you if I can come right now.

Now write your own sentences using **ask** and **tell**.

1. _____

2. _____

Barely

Use **barely** when there's nothing left over.

Don't use **barely** when it's close in time.

*Example of what **not** to say:*
He **barely** left for Alaska.

Just

Use **just** if it's close in time.

Example:
He **just** left for Alaska.

Practice: Write **barely** or **just** in the spaces below.

Hi, Mrs. O'Brien. Can you tell Soledad that I _____ got
1

home? I _____ have time to do my homework before we
2

leave. Can she wait 15 minutes? That will be _____ enough
3

time to do my math. No it won't. Tell you what. I'll call again

_____ before I'm finished. What? She just left? Well, I can see
4

I'm _____ going to make it through this day.
5

Write **barely** or **just** in the spaces below. Use **barely** when there's nothing left over; use just if it's close in time.

1. I had _____ finished the first page when he called.

2. He is _____ over two feet tall.

3. He could _____ get the shirt buttoned.

4. She _____ arrived this minute.

5. The fire was very hot, but he was _____ burned at all.

6. The zoo keepers _____ got here a minute ago.

7. The elephant _____ touched her, if he did at all.

8. That was exciting. I can _____ breathe.

9. The store is _____ two minutes from here.

10. The pizza is _____ even warm.

11. I ate so much I can _____ stand up.

12. We _____ finished eating.

Now write your own sentences using **barely** and **just**.

1. _____

2. _____

Borrow

Use **borrow** when you mean the person receiving.

Example:
I'll ask him if I can **borrow** his pen.

Loan

Use **loan** when you mean the person giving.

Example:
I'll ask him if he will **loan** me a pen.

Practice: Write **borrow** or **loan** in the spaces below.

Person 1:   Will you _____ me two dollars?
                              1

Person 2:   No, man. I _____ed you five dollars last week, and you didn't
                            2

              pay it back.

Person 1:   Aw, come on! I just want to _____ a couple more.
                                            3

Person 2:   You say _____, but I think you mean take.
                          4

Person 1:   I'm just asking you to _____ me a few bucks. I'll pay you back.
                                        5

Person 2:   Sorry. I _____, you keep. You don't _____. You mooch.
                          6   7

Borrow and Loan • Practice

Write **borrow** or **loan** in the spaces below. Remember, if you need something, you **borrow**. If someone needs something from you, you **loan**.

1. We can _____ money from the bank.

2. The bank will probably approve the _____.

3. If you'll make me a loan, I'll never ask to _____ from you again.

4. May I _____ your horse?

5. I never _____ out my rooster.

6. Will a pawn shop _____ me money?

7. I don't like to _____ things from people.

8. You want me to _____ you a cup of sugar?

9. The dentist says I shouldn't _____ anyone else's toothbrush.

10. Somebody told me I shouldn't _____ my hairbrush to people.

Now write your own sentences using **borrow** and **loan**.

1. _____

2. _____

English
I Missed

Brake

Use **brake** if you mean stopping.

Example:
Put your foot on the **brake**!

Break

Use **break** when something is divided into pieces.

Example:
Break the egg.

Practice: Write **brake** or **break** in the spaces below.

If I _____ up with him, it will _____ his heart. But he scares me. I have
    1   2

seen him _____ things when he is mad. Sometimes he doesn't _____ at
          3   4

stop lights. He thinks it's real funny to pretend the _____s went out. I think
                                                       5

he's out of control. I also think if I _____ up with him it might save my life.
                                        6

Brake and Break • Practice

Write **brake** or **break** in the spaces below. Use **brake** when you are talking about stopping; use **break** the rest of the time.

1. Slam on the _____ s!

2. _____ is at 3:00.

3. The priest tells us to _____ bread.

4. Let's have _____ fast.

5. How did you _____ your leg?

6. _____ it in half.

7. The right _____ on my bicycle is broken.

8. He _____s down and cries like a baby.

9. _____ it up!

10. Your _____s are gone.

11. I _____ things down to understand them better.

12. He says, "Give me a _____."

Now write your own sentences using **brake** and **break**.

1. _____

2. _____

Can

Use **can** when you have the ability.

Example:
I **can** come over Thursday.

May

Use **may** when something might happen, or to ask permission.

Example:
May I come over Thursday?

Practice: Write **can** or **may** in the spaces below.

I got my paycheck today. I am rich! It's a good feeling to know I _____ pay my

1

bills. After that, I _____ still buy some things I want. I _____ even have

2   3

a few dollars left for my nephew. If I _____ keep myself from using my

4

whole paycheck today, I _____ save some money for later. I think I

5

_____ buy a car this way. I _____ even take a trip to Vietnam!

6   7

Can and May • Practice

Write **can** or **may** in the spaces below. Use **can** when you are talking about ability; use **may** when something is possible.

1. _____ I sit down?

2. _____ I join you?

3. _____ you find the toothpaste?

4. I _____ decide to go home if it gets too dark.

5. I _____ count from one to ten.

6. Happy Hats Company. _____ I help you?

7. I _____ help you.

8. I _____ picture the lake and all the trees.

9. I _____ picture the mosquitoes running now!

10. You _____ be able to because you've been watching too many cartoons.

11. _____ I help you cross the street?

Now write your own sentences using **can** and **may**.

1. _____

2. _____

Cause

Use **cause** if you mean the reason that something happens.

Example:
Too much rain in a short time can **cause** a flood.

Because

Use **because** (**not 'cause**) in writing standard English.

Example:
It is flooding **because** of all the rain.

Practice: Write **cause** or **because** in the spaces below.

My grandma says I'm overweight _____ my aunts are overweight. But
                                    1

the _____ could be chips. I eat chips _____ I like them. While I am
       2   3

eating, I tell myself that chips don't _____ me to gain weight. After I eat
                                          4

them, I realize that they probably do. I think I'll stop eating chips to see if they are

the _____ _____ it could be a defective bathing suit.
       5   6

Cause and Because • Practice

Write **cause** or **because** in the spaces below. Remember, **cause** is the reason something happens, and **because** (**not 'cause**) is the conjunction to use in standard English writing.

1. What is the _____ of wars?

2. _____ they forgot about the effects of violence, they fought again.

3. My dog wags her tail _____ she's friendly.

4. Lipstick can _____ stains.

5. I sing _____ I'm happy.

6. Does heat always _____ light?

7. Does she know the _____?

8. I trust her _____ we're friends.

9. Does dirt _____ sun spots?

10. Does the sun _____ freckles?

11. Does thunder _____ lightning?

12. I ask _____ I don't know.

Now write your own sentences using **cause** and **because**.

1. _____

2. _____

Close

Don't use **close** when you mean to **turn** or **shut off**.

*Example of what **not** to say:*
Close the lights.

Turn/Shut Off

Use **turn off** the lights or **shut off** the lights.

Practice: Write **close, turn off,** or **shut off** in the spaces below.

When I feel like dreaming, I _____ my eyes. I ask my sister to

1

_____ the radio. I ask my brothers to _____ the TV. If it's

2   3

nighttime, I _____ the lights. Then I _____ my door. Do you dream,

4   5

too?

Close and Turn/Shut Off • Practice

Write **close, turn off,** or **shut off** in the spaces below. Remember, you can't close a light, the radio, or TV.

1. Is it okay to _____ the lights?

2. He'll need to _____ the water.

3. _____ your eyes.

4. I forgot to _____ the gate.

5. Did you _____ the cable service?

6. Please _____ the lights.

7. Does the light _____ when you close the refrigerator door?

8. Let's _____ the lights and tell scary stories.

9. You can _____ the flashlight.

10. Did you _____ the lights in all the rooms?

11. They had to _____ up the shop.

12. Please _____ the gas!

Now write your own sentences using **close** and **turn off** or **shut off.**

1. _____

2. _____

Doesn't with no

Don't use **doesn't** with no.

Example of what __not__ to say:
She **doesn't** eat no meat.

Doesn't with any

Use **doesn't** with any.

Example:
She **doesn't** eat any meat.

Or use **no** alone.

Example:
She eats **no** meat.

Practice: Write **any** or **no** in the spaces below.

I am a vegetarian. I eat _____ beef or chicken. However, I have _____
                                  1   2

problem with eating fish. Okay, so I'm 50 percent vegetarian. I also love ice

cream. (A true vegetarian doesn't eat or drink _____ food that comes
                                                                3

from an animal.) Here's a better idea. I'm a 100 percent individual who just

doesn't eat _____ beef or chicken.
                        4

Doesn't with No and Any • Practice

Write **no** or **any** in the spaces below. Remember, don't use two negative words **(not and no)** together.

1. She doesn't have measles _____ more.

2. He doesn't want _____ vegetables.

3. It has _____ damage.

4. There doesn't seem to be _____ work to do.

5. She doesn't like to wear _____ jewelry.

6. It looks like there are _____ Twix™ left.

7. He doesn't have _____ debts at all.

8. He doesn't owe _____ money to _____ one.

9. It doesn't rain _____ more.

10. He doesn't come by _____ more.

11. She gets _____ cable at her house.

12. It doesn't get that hot _____ more.

Now write your own sentence using **doesn't** with **any**.

1. _____

Doesn't with none

Don't use **doesn't** with **none**.

Example of what not to use:
He **doesn't** have **none**.

Doesn't with any

Use **doesn't** with **any**.

Example:
He **doesn't** have **any**.

Or use **none** alone.

Example:
He has **none**.

Practice: Write **none** or **any** in the spaces below.

We are having a raffle for our club. Sheila sold ten tickets

today. She has _____ left. Joe says he has _____ left,
$_1$ ... $_2$

either. Ricky doesn't have _____ yet, and he will do well once he
$_3$

starts. Is there _____ reason we might fail to meet our goal?
$_4$

There doesn't seem to be _____ at all.
$_5$

Doesn't with None and Any • Practice

Write **none** or **any** in the spaces below. Remember, don't use two negatives **(not and none)** together.

1. He doesn't have _____ either.

2. My school doesn't have _____.

3. She doesn't plant _____.

4. I'd say he has _____ to sell.

5. Yours needs some, but mine needs _____.

6. Their daughter has _____.

7. My car doesn't need _____.

8. This boat doesn't carry _____.

9. There are _____ on this list.

10. Did she eat _____ of that?

11. Doesn't he have _____.

12. Doesn't it show _____?

Now write your own sentence using **doesn't** with **any**.

1. _____

Doesn't with Nothing and Anything

Doesn't with Nothing

Don't use **doesn't** with **nothing**.

Example of what not to say:
She **doesn't** want **nothing**.

Doesn't with Anything

Use **doesn't** with **anything**.

Example:
She **doesn't** want **anything** right now.

Or use **nothing** alone.

Example:
She wants **nothing** right now.

Practice: Write **nothing** or **anything** in the spaces below.

I have _____ to write with. Oh, thanks. I'll return it when I'm finished.

1

Now I don't have _____ to write on. Wow, thanks. Now I don't have

2

_____ to write about. I guess I don't have to borrow _____

3   4

after all. I have _____ to do.

5

Write **nothing** or **anything** in the spaces below. Remember, don't use two negative words **(not and nothing)** together.

1. He has _____ to worry about.

2. It doesn't have _____ to do with anything.

3. Doesn't _____ bother her?

4. He feels like he has _____ to look forward to.

5. He never does _____ alone.

6. Doesn't _____ ever happen around here?

7. This shirt doesn't go with _____ in my closet.

8. The remote control doesn't do _____.

9. This book doesn't say _____ about the Vietnam war.

10. That wire doesn't connect with _____.

11. Won't _____ ever change?

12. The book says _____ about the war.

Now write your own sentence using **doesn't** with **anything**.

1. _____

Don't

Don't use   <u>he don't</u>

          <u>she don't</u>

          <u>it don't</u>

Doesn't

Use   <u>he doesn't</u>

          <u>she doesn't</u>

          <u>it doesn't</u>

Practice: Write <u>don't</u> or <u>doesn't</u> in the spaces below.

His wife _____ like peas. He _____ like squash. She _____
        1   2   3

like carrots. He _____ like broccoli. They _____ eat many vegetables
               4   5

at all. He says it _____ matter, but he _____ know for sure. She
                 6   7

says she _____want to change her mind about cooked vegetables, but she
        8

_____ think she would mind carrot juice. She _____ know for sure.
9   10

Don't and Doesn't • Practice

Write **don't** or **doesn't** in the spaces below. Remember how to use the verb *to do*: I, you, we, and they **don't;** he, she, and it **doesn't.**

1. That sweater _____ go with those pants.

2. Those socks _____ go well together.

3. He _____ go out much.

4. _____ the sun feel great?

5. Summertime seems very short, _____ it?

6. She _____ care what other people think.

7. That beats all, _____ it?

8. They _____ always answer their phone.

9. She _____ know what to say.

10. He _____ care about schooling.

11. It _____ matter to him.

12. _____ you know he's getting married?

Now write your own sentences using **don't** and **doesn't.**

1. _____

2. _____

Don't have to

Don't use **don't have to** if you mean something is forbidden.

Example of what not to say:
Police officers **don't have to** drink alcohol on the job.

Use   **not supposed to**

             not allowed to

             must not

Examples:
I'm **not supposed to** be out after 11:00.
Children are **not allowed to** go in without an adult.
We absolutely **must not** go in.

Practice: Write **not supposed to, not allowed to,** or **must not** in the spaces below.

It seems to me that there are many rules in life. People in some religions are

_____ dance. In many schools, students are _____ be
1   2

in the hall without a pass. More and more companies tell employees they

absolutely_____ use drugs on the job. Even I have a rule:
        3

My brothers and sisters _____ use my stuff.
                4

Write **not supposed to**, **not allowed to**, or **must not** in the spaces below. Remember, use **don't have to** only when you mean something is not required.

1. You _____ eat that if you don't like it.

2. You _____ drive without a license.

3. You _____ go in there, if you don't want to.

4. You _____ bring beer into the ballpark.

5. You're _____ go in there.

6. If you are too tired, you _____ try to swim the channel.

7. We are _____ smoke on campus.

8. Convicted felons are _____ vote.

9. His doctor says he absolutely _____ eat fat.

Now write your own sentences using **not supposed to**, **not allowed to**, and **must not**.

1. _____

2. _____

3. _____

Don't with no

Don't use **don't** with **no**.

*Example of what **not** to say:*
I **don't** want **no** hair gel.

Don't with any

Use **don't** with **any**.

Example:
I **don't** want **any** hair gel.

Or use **no** alone.

Example:
I want **no** hair gel on my hair.

Practice: Write **no** or **any** in the spaces below.

When I don't have _____ hair gel, I have _____ hairstyle. You see some girls
          1   2

who don't wear _____ lipstick. Some girls wear _____ mascara. I don't
          3   4

criticize any other styles, but I don't go out if I don't have _____ gel. I have my
                                                5

own style: jeans, T-shirt, and hair gel.

Don't with No and Any • Practice

Write **no** or **any** in the spaces below. Remember, don't use two negative words **(not and no)** together.

1. We have _____ more time.

2. They don't need _____ more furniture.

3. Why don't you want _____ potatoes?

4. I don't have _____ appetite.

5. Don't eat _____ more candy!

6. We have _____ boys in our class!

7. I don't want to sing in front of _____ boys.

8. Don't they sell _____ used cars?

9. We don't have _____ gas.

10. I have _____ homework.

11. They don't want _____ trouble.

Now write your own sentences using **don't** with **any,** and **no** without **don't.**

1. _____

2. _____

Don't with none

Don't use **don't** with **none**.

Example of what not to say:
I don't want **none**.

Don't with any

Use **don't** with **any**.

Example:
I **don't** want any of these.

Or use **none** alone.

Example:
I want **none** of these.

Practice: Write **none** or **any** in the spaces below.

I don't want _____ fries. I don't need _____ dessert. You might wonder why
        1   2

I'm here. I'm here because I'm hungry. But I have no money. _____ . I'm going
                                                                3

home. _____ of the food at home costs money. Well, it doesn't cost *me* money.
         4

Don't with None and Any • Practice

Write **none** or **any** in the spaces below. Remember, don't use two negative words **(not and none)** together.

1. I have _____ at all.

2. These rooms don't have _____.

3. I don't see _____.

4. You saved _____ for me!

5. I don't think I'll give you _____.

6. They don't make _____ of these.

7. Don't put _____ in the paper bag.

8. Most classrooms don't have _____.

9. Don't buy _____ for me.

10. We don't ever use _____, thank you.

11. I still don't see _____.

Now write your own sentences using **don't** with **any**, or **none** without **don't**.

1. _____

2. _____

Don't with Nothing and Anything

Don't with nothing

Don't use **don't** with **nothing**.

Example of what <u>not</u> to use:
I don't want **nothing** to do with it.

Don't with anything

Use **don't** with **anything**.

Example:
I **don't** want **anything** to do with it.

Or use **nothing** alone.

Example:
I had **nothing** to do with it.

Practice: Write **nothing** or **anything** in the spaces below.

I babysit my little cousin. I always ask, "What are you doing?" He says,

"_____." I say, "Come on, tell me what you're doing!" He says he's

1

not doing _____. Then I go into his room. He really isn't doing

2

_____. "Come into the living room," I tell him. "There isn't

3

_____ to do in there," he says. "Well," I say, "if there is _____

4   5

to do, do it out here!"

Write **nothing** or **anything** in the spaces below. Remember, don't use two negative words **(not and nothing)** together.

1. I have _____ to wear.

2. They don't do _____ much except watch TV.

3. We don't need _____ else.

4. We have _____ to do while we're waiting.

5. Don't you ever need _____?

6. We don't ever keep _____ from you.

7. I don't remember _____!

8. I forget _____.

9. Don't you want _____ from the store?

10. I don't feel _____ when you pinch me.

11. Do you like _____?

Now write your own sentence using **don't** with **anything**, or **nothing** without **don't**.

1. _____

2. _____

Either

Use **either** to mean one or the other.

Example:
I'll buy **either** chocolate or strawberry.

Neither

Use: **neither** to mean *not either one.*

Example:
Neither one sounds good to me.

Practice: Write **either** or **neither** in the spaces below.

_____ you or I have to decide what flavor to buy. You don't like
1

strawberry? Me _____. _____ of us likes vanilla. Let's go to
2   3

_____ 31 Flavors or the other ice cream store. Then we can get
4

_____ Cookies and Cream or Peanut Butter, which are flavors we
5

both like.

Either and Neither • Practice

Write **either** or **neither** in the spaces below. Remember, use **either** if you mean one or the other. Use **neither** if you mean *not either one.*

1. Mom's gone to _____ the store or her class.

2. Both are wrong. _____ one is correct.

3. _____ of us has a dime!

4. He said he didn't want to go, and I said, "Me _____."

5. We could see _____ an action movie or a romantic one.

6. The report isn't on _____ TV or radio.

7. _____ the apples nor the plums look fresh.

8. I can't find _____ one!

9. If you're not going, I'm not going _____.

10. Get me _____ a rag or a towel, quick!

11. He's not going swimming and _____ is she.

Now write your own sentences using **either** and **neither.**

1. _____

2. _____

Else

Use **else** when you mean something different or something besides.

Example:
I am out of Pepsi. Would you like something **else**?

More

Use **more** to talk about a greater amount of something.

Example:
Would you like **more** Pepsi?

Practice: Write **else** or **more** in the spaces below.

I've used up all my shampoo. I like the brand, so I will probably buy _____.

1

But I am also thinking about trying something _____ . My friend likes shampoo

2

with conditioner _____ than regular shampoo. Now I have a big hairy decision:

3

get _____ of what I've been using, or buy something _____, like what she

4   5

uses.

Else and More • Practice

Write **else** or **more** in the spaces below. Use **else** when you mean some other thing; use **more** when you want an additional amount.

1. Do you want _____ spaghetti?

2. Do you want something _____ with your spaghetti?

3. It isn't working. What _____ shall I try?

4. There is _____ to the story.

5. There is something _____ that I haven't told you.

6. Tell me _____.

7. Try _____ of the same.

8. Let's play this game some _____.

9. Let's play something _____ instead.

10. I'll buy you something _____ that fits!

11. Switch to something _____.

12. Try something _____.

Now write your own sentences using **else** and **more.**

1. _____

2. _____

Every Time

Use **every time** to emphasize the parts.

Example:
I go to the movies **every time** I have money.

All the Time

Use **all the time** to emphasize the whole.

Example:
I go to the movies **all the time**.

Practice: Write **every time** or **all the time** in the spaces below.

_____ I go to my friend's house, she is babysitting. She says she

1

doesn't really babysit _____. But _____ I go there, she is!

2   3

She says _____ I come, her mother is at work. Well, it seems to

4

me that her mother must work _____. My friend says I eat

5

_____. So I guess we both think the other does one

6

thing _____.

7

Write **every time** or **all the time** in the spaces below. Think of **every time** as every *single* time; think of **all the time** as the *total*.

1. _____ I start to study, the phone rings.

2. The phone rings _____ .

3. _____ we get a phone bill, I pay.

4. She comes over _____ I'm sleeping.

5. _____ I visit, you're eating macaroni and cheese.

6. He drinks coffee _____.

7. I'm in a hurry _____.

8. _____ I come home, he's waiting for me.

9. She wears earrings _____.

10. He wears a hat _____ he goes out.

11. _____ I come over, you are so nice to me.

Now write your own sentences using **every time** and **all the time**.

1. _____

2. _____

Feel

Use **feel** when you mean a touch or an emotion.

Example:
I can **feel** the wet paint.

Example:
I **feel** fine.

Fell

Use **fell** when you mean the past of *to fall.*

Example:
Yesterday, I **fell** down.

Practice: Write **feel** or **fell** in the spaces below.

She _____ and bumped her head. When she got up, she said, "I don't _____
    1   2

well. Should I lie down for a while?" Her friend said, "When I _____ sick, I eat
                                                                         3

ice cream." "Well," she said, "I am sure I _____ hard enough for ice cream!
                                                    4

I _____ better already."
    5

Feel and Fell • Practice

Write **feel** or **fell** in the spaces below. Remember, use **feel** to talk about the senses and your feelings; use **fell** to talk about something that just became a victim of gravity.

1. I'm telling you, I _____ fine.

2. How do you _____?

3. He _____ in the lion's cage and was mauled.

4. She _____ off her bike and into the ice plant.

5. The stunt man _____ ten stories without a net.

6. Do you _____ that bump?

7. I want to _____ good about what I do.

8. Don't you care about my _____ings?

9. How do you _____, Mr. Seal?

10. His keys _____ down the hotel well.

11. He felt happy when he _____ in love.

12. I just _____ that it's a good deal.

Now write your own sentences using **feel** and **fell.**

1. _____

2. _____

For

Use **for** to show a purpose.

Example:
I am going to the kitchen **for** more food.

Because

Use **because** to show a reason or result.

Example:
I am eating **because** I am hungry.

Practice: Write **for** or **because** in the spaces below.

My girlfriend is applying _____ a student loan. She is going to the
₁

community college _____ they have a good nursing program. I am
₂

going _____ I want to be a teacher. We didn't study much in high
₃

school _____ we just wanted to party. We're going to study in
₄

college so that we can get all the credits we need _____ a college degree.
₅

Write **for** or **because** in the sentences below. Remember, use **for** to show the intention; use **because** to show the result.

1. I dance _____ I like to.

2. Take the umbrella _____ it's raining.

3. They'll hold together _____ they're stapled.

4. She likes plastic wrap _____ she can see through it.

5. It's padlocked _____ security.

6. We'll eat indoors _____ it's so hot.

7. Pencils are good _____ you can erase mistakes.

8. I'm staying _____ I'm too tired to drive.

9. I'm going to the store _____ a newspaper.

10. I sing _____ I'm a music major.

11. I want to go home now _____ I am finished.

Now write your own sentences using **for** and **because.**

1. _____

2. _____

For

Don't use **for** when you mean *because*.

Example of what <u>not</u> to say:
She wears nice clothes **for** he will notice her.

So

Use **so** if you want to show why.

Example:
She wears nice clothes **so** that he will notice her.

Or use **for** like this: She wears nice clothes **for** him.

Practice: Write **for** or **so** in the spaces below.

I take the bus to work every day. I have to be on time _____ that the bus will not

1

leave without me. I buy a bus pass _____ that I can save money. I plan to buy a

2

car _____ that I can make my own schedule. My friend rides the bus, too. He is

3

saving his money _____ car insurance! We both work _____ that, hopefully

4   5

soon, we can drive our cars to work!

Write **for** or **so** in the spaces below. Remember, use **so** if you mean *because*.

1. I went _____ that I could see him.

2. I am saving money _____ a sofa.

3. He works out _____ that he can be strong.

4. I will buy new shoes _____ my graduation.

5. She is going home now _____ that she can make dinner.

6. He registers early _____ that he can get good classes.

7. I go early _____ that I can get back early.

8. Take a dollar _____ that you can have a key made.

9. Would you remove your laundry _____ that I can use the washer?

10. I bought cologne _____ that I can smell good.

11. We got cable _____ the fights.

12. He likes to eat protein _____ that he can feel energetic all day.

Now write your own sentences using **for** and **so**.

1. _____

2. _____

Go Walking

Don't use I **have to go walking** if you mean how you get somewhere.

*Example of what **not** to say:*
I'm going to be late to school because I have to go **walking**.

Walk

Use I have to **walk**.

Example:
I have to **walk** to school.

Or use **go walking** or **walk** when it is something you do for exercise or fun.

Practice: Write **go walking** or **walk** in the spaces below.

Last year, I had to _____ to work, so I got up very early. Then I
                        1

took the bus. But I still got up early to_____to the bus stop. I bought
                                            2

a car so I could sleep in! Then my friend said we should exercise more. So now I

get up very early to _____ with my friend.
                        3

Write **go walking** or **walk** in the spaces below.

1. How far do you _____ to your bus stop?

2. Many people _____ in the park for exercise.

3. My dad had to _____two miles to school!

4. Let's _____ in the rain!

5. Do I have to _____ all the way to the store again?

6. He lost his license, so he has to _____ wherever he goes.

7. I have to _____ home today.

8. Do we have to _____ everywhere at Disneyland, or is there a tram?

9. They decided to _____ to the movies.

10. How long will it take you to _____ here?

Now write your own sentences using **go walking** and **walk**.

1. _____

2. _____

Gonna

Don't use **gonna**.

Why not? It is not standard English.

Going To

Use **going to**.

Example:
I'm **going to** do that.

Practice: Write **going to** or **not going to** in the spaces below.

I'm _____ do everything! I'm _____ sky dive. I'm
‎   1   2

_____ deep sea dive. I'm _____ snow board, and I'm
  3   4

_____ water ski. I'm _____ France. I'm _____
  5   6   7

China. I'm _____ be rich, and I'm _____ give lots of money
‎   8   9

to feed the hungry. I'm _____ miss a single good thing.
‎   10

Gonna and Going To • Practice

Write **going to** or **not going to** in the sentences below. Remember, *gonna* isn't standard English.

1. We're _____ have ice cream.

2. No, my dog is _____ have puppies; she's just fat!

3. I'm _____ eat until I'm stuffed.

4. Watch out! You're _____ trip.

5. He's working late, so he's _____ get home in time.

6. They're all _____ dye their hair.

7. The power is out, so the lights are _____ come back on very soon.

8. Everyone's _____ want to go.

9. Are you _____ have your hair cut on Saturday?

10. What are you _____ do about Arnold?

11. Do you think that tree is _____ fall on the roof?

12. What are you _____ do about it?

Now write your own sentences using **going to** and **not going to**.

1. _____

2. _____

Got

Don't use I don't **got**.

Have

Use I don't **have** or I haven't **got**.

Example:
I **don't have** my credit card and **haven't got** any cash.

Practice: Write **got** or **have** in the spaces below.

I have a cold, but I don't _____ a telephone to call in sick. I don't want to go to
₁

work, but I don't _____ a fever. I could go to Six Flags, but I don't _____ any
₂ ₃

money. I'll get oranges. I'll go to work. I haven't _____ that many germs.
₄

I don't _____ a good reason to stay home.
₅

Got and Have • Practice

Write **<u>got</u>** or **<u>have</u>** in the spaces below. Remember, **<u>got</u>** doesn't go with **<u>don't</u>** or **<u>doesn't</u>**.

1. I don't _____ a car.

2. She doesn't _____ twelve cats.

3. He hasn't _____ the money.

4. They don't _____ rabies.

5. We don't _____ any lettuce.

6. My grandparents don't _____ five children.

7. I haven't _____ my paycheck yet.

8. It doesn't _____ to be that expensive.

9. Do I _____ to go?

10. I don't _____ time.

11. He doesn't _____ running shoes.

12. I haven't _____plans.

Now write your own sentences using **<u>got</u>** and **<u>have</u>**.

1. _____

2. _____

Of

Don't use I would **of** gone.

Have

Use   I would **have** gone.

       I should **have** done that.

       I could **have** made it.

       I might **have** had fun.

Of indicates a fact about something.

Example:
I should have a pocket full **of** money tomorrow.

Practice: Write **would have**, **should have**, **could have**, **might have**, or **of** in the spaces below.

It _____ been better if we had won. We _____ had a big old
    1   2

trophy. We _____ gotten more sleep instead _____ staying
              3   4

out so late. Then we _____ been heroes.
                     5

Of and Have • Practice

Write **of** or **have** in the sentences below.

1. He bought a bag _____ peanuts.

2. He would _____ come, but he didn't have a ride.

3. We thought you would _____ left by now.

4. They should _____ eaten without you.

5. It could _____ been better.

6. We have a government _____ the people, by the people, and for the people.

7. If it's 8:00, he will _____ already picked her up.

8. He might _____ called.

9. You can't _____ spent it all already!

10. I could _____ had orange juice.

11. I should _____ taken the bus.

12. We should _____ asked.

Now write your own sentences using **of** and **have**.

1. _____

2. _____

He's

Use **he's** when you mean **he is** or **he has**.

Example:
He's the greatest!

His

Use **his** when you mean something belongs to **him**.

Example:
His room is stuffed with **his** awards.

Practice: Write **he's** or **his** in the spaces below.

_____ not the only basketball player in his family. _____ big sister plays on the
₁   ₂

varsity team. She says _____ her biggest fan. He says she's _____ biggest
                        ₃   ₄

competition! _____ best score in a game is 18. Her best score is 22! He says
            ₅

_____ learned many pointers from his sister. She says _____ the best kid she
₆   ₇

has ever trained.

He's and His • Practice

Write **he's** or **his** in the spaces below. Use **he's** when you mean *he is*; use **his** when you are referring to someone's possession.

1. What's _____ name?

2. Where is _____ backpack?

3. It's _____ business, not ours.

4. _____ parents are proud that he is going to graduate.

5. He says _____ _____ own worst enemy.

6. _____ late.

7. _____ got a baseball card collection and a signed basketball.

8. He has _____ name carved in the sidewalk.

9. What's _____ problem?

10. _____ crazy about math.

11. _____ brother is crazy about science.

12. _____ supposed to help us, _____ best friends.

Now write your own sentences using **he's** and **his**.

1. _____

2. _____

English I Missed

I Don't Mind

Don't use **I don't mind** when someone offers you something.

Example of what <u>not</u> to say:
Person 1: Would you like a ride home?
Person 2: **I don't mind**.

Use   **I'd like that**.

      I would appreciate that.

      Yes, thank you.

Example:
Person 1: Would you like a ride home?
Person 2: **Yes, thank you**!

Or use **I don't mind** this way:

Person 1: May I go before you?
Person 2: **I don't mind**.

Practice: Write **I'd like that** or **I don't mind** in the spaces below.

Person 1:   Can you come over to my house?

Person 2:   _____, but I might have to bring my nephew.
               1

Person 1:   _____ .
               2

Person 2:   I warn you. He can be very noisy!

Person 1:   It's okay. _____ noise.
               3

I Don't Mind • Practice

Write **I'd like that** or **I don't mind** in the spaces below.

1. Person 1: Would you go out with me?

   Person 2: _____ , thank you.

2. Person 1: Do you want some iced tea?

   Person 2: _____ , thank you.

3. Person 1: Will it bother you if I turn on the TV?

   Person 2: _____ .

4. Person 1: Doesn't all the traffic bother you?

   Person 2: _____ .

5. Person 1: Let's go watch the sunset.

   Person 2: _____ .

Now write your own conversations using **I'd like that** and **I don't mind**.

1. Person 1: _____.

   Person 2: _____.

2. Person 1: _____.

   Person 2: _____.

Its

Use **its** when you want to show possession.

Example:
What is **its** name?

It's

Use **it's** when you mean *it is*.

Example:
It's a nice day.

Practice: Write **its** or **it's** in the spaces below.

Person 1:   Hurry up! _____ time for the movie to begin.
                          1

Person 2:   I am! Hey, you never told me _____ name!
                                            2

Person 1:   I forget, but I know _____ good.
                                   3

Person 2:   Who said?

Person 1:   All _____ reviews are great.
                  4

Person 2:   Do you know anyone who has seen it?

Person 1:   Trust me. _____ reviews are great and _____ time to go!
                        5   6

Its and It's • Practice

Write **its** or **it's** in the spaces below. Remember, use **its** when something belongs to something; use **it's** when you mean *it is*.

1. _____ my turn.

2. Where do you think _____ going?

3. What's _____ name?

4. _____ hot outside.

5. I like _____ color.

6. We don't think _____ okay.

7. Where is _____ door?

8. Do you like _____ shape?

9. _____ still in _____ shell.

10. Where is _____ warranty?

11. I said, " _____ mine."

12. _____ happening.

Now write your own sentences using **its** and **it's**.

1. _____

2. _____

Just

Use **just** when you mean the very recent past.

Example:
She **just** left a minute ago.

Right Now

Use **right now** to emphasize the present.

Example:
She is leaving **right now**!

Practice: Write **just** or **right now** in the spaces below.

Person 1: Hi! I was _____ leaving when the phone rang.
                                    1

Person 2: You're leaving _____ ? Has Junior gone?
                                          2

Person 1: He _____ left.
                        3

Person 1: Is Pookie there?

Person 2: Yes. She's leaving with me. Sorry, I have to hang up.

           Our ride's probably waiting outside _____.
                                                                    4

Person 1: No. I'm your ride, and I'm leaving _____ to pick you up.
                                                                5

Just and Right Now • Practice

Write **just** or **right now** in the spaces below. Remember, use **just** for something that happened in the very recent past; use **right now** to emphasize the present.

1. They should turn the lights on _____ .

2. They _____ turned the lights on.

3. The game is starting _____ .

4. The game _____ started.

5. She _____ left.

6. She is leaving _____ .

7. The festival is ending _____ .

8. The festival _____ ended.

9. He called _____ this minute.

10. He is calling _____ .

11. I am going to work _____ .

12. I got to work _____ a minute ago.

Now write your own sentences using **just** and **right now**.

1. _____

2. _____

Left To

Don't use He **left to** Mexico.

You can say: He **left to** lock up the store.

Use   He **left for** Mexico.

or   He **left to go to** Mexico.

Practice: Write **left for**, **left to go to**, or **left to** in the spaces below.

My family has _____ check out the Corn Festival. We all went last year.

¹

This time I have to work. In fact, I should have _____ work by this time!

²

However, I'll try to come to the festival tonight after work. Anyway, you don't

want to miss any of it. You should have _____ the festival a half

³

hour ago, so hurry!

Write **left for**, **left to go to**, or **left to** in the spaces below. Remember, you don't say, "We left to" somewhere in standard English.

1. She _____ the market.

2. They _____ Guadalajara.

3. He _____ see if his wallet is at the bus station.

4. Yesterday, I _____ work without my wallet.

5. We _____ school a little early today.

6. He _____ water the lawn at his grandpa's house.

7. I thought you _____ the ball park.

8. She _____ the dentist.

9. We _____ pick her up at the airport at 6:30 A.M.

10. The cable installer has already _____ our house.

11. They _____ the field trip already.

Now write your own sentences using **left for** and **left to go to**.

1. _____

2. _____

Less

Use **less** when you are not thinking about numbers.

Example:
I want **less** milk. (You **can't** count milk.)

Fewer

Use **fewer** when you *are* thinking about numbers.

Example:
I want **fewer** glasses of milk. (You **can** count glasses.)

Practice: Write **less** or **fewer** in the spaces below.

Your cats are _____ trouble than my cats. And I have _____ cats!
1   2

I suspect that all of mine are spoiled. Do you think I should give my cats

_____ attention? Maybe _____ treats would help. I am certain that if I
3   4

change some things, I will have _____hassle with my cats.
                                             5

Less and Fewer • Practice

Write **less** or **fewer** in the spaces below. Remember, if you can count something, use **fewer**.

1. I have _____ hair now than I did last week.

2. I have _____ credit cards than I used to.

3. Having _____ bills means I spend less money on stamps.

4. They gave you _____ salad than they gave me.

5. Maybe it's just that I have _____ carrots in mine.

6. I have a few _____ than I need.

7. She has _____ quarters than I do.

8. Overall, I have _____ coins than she has.

9. _____ is more.

10. It'll take _____ time because we have _____ math problems.

11. Are there _____ people here than last year?

12. No, we just have _____ noise.

Now write your own sentences using **less** and **fewer**.

1. _____

2. _____

English
I Missed

Life

Don't use our **lifes**.

Lives

Use our **lives**.

Why? It's one **life**, but two or more **lives**.

Practice: Write **life** or **lives** in the spaces below.

"One _____ to Live" is a TV soap opera. It's not really about one _____. It's
     1   2

about many _____. All my sisters watch it. They plan their _____ around it.
           3   4

I think the title really means that we all have one _____ and we should live
               5

it well. So isn't it funny that my sisters spend their _____ thinking about a soap
               6

opera that is telling them to, well, get a _____?
               7

Write **life** or **lives** in the spaces below. Remember, its one **life**, two **lives**.

1. I have my whole _____ ahead of me.

2. They say cats have nine _____.

3. Many _____ were saved today.

4. We've been friends all our _____.

5. Do you believe in past _____?

6. The _____ of some people are much different from others.

7. My _____ will be much better now.

8. All of our _____ will be much better now.

Life/lives is like **knife/knives**, **calf/calve**s, **wolf/wolves**, and **shelf/shelves**. Try these. Write the correct word in the spaces below.

9. They were howling like _____.

10. I need some _____ for books in my bedroom.

11. We don't have any sharp _____ at my house.

12. The _____ are running loose on the freeway.

13. Our friends' _____ are important to us.

Tall

Use **tall** only if you're measuring something from the ground up to the sky.

Example:
He is very **tall**.

Long

Use **long** for other measurements that are just from end to end.

Example:
The branch is very **long**.

Practice: Write **long** or **tall** in the spaces below.

The queen of Jordan is named Noor. She is very _____.
                                                    1

Her clothes are too _____ for most women to wear. Queen Noor is married to
                    2

King Hussein, who is not as _____ as she is, but very respected.
                            3

The Jordanians hope to have their beloved king and _____ queen for a
                                                   4

_____ time.
5

Write **long** or **tall** in the spaces below. Remember, **long** is used to describe length, **tall** for height.

1. My nose is too _____.

2. Look how _____ the elephant's ears are!

3. I like _____ grain rice.

4. In the field, corn grows very _____.

5. How _____ is your hair?

6. How _____ are you?

7. Your fingers are _____.

8. Why are telephone poles so _____?

9. The curtains are too _____ for the windows.

10. I like to drink cold water in a _____ cold glass.

11. Your son is _____ for his age.

Now write your own sentences using **long** and **tall**.

1. _____

2. _____

Lose

Use **lose** when you mean failing to keep something.

Example:
I **lose** my keys all the time.

Loose

Use **loose** when something isn't tight, or is free to move.

Example:
My shoelace is **loose** (not tight).

Example:
Let's let the dog **loose** (be free).

Practice: Write **lose** or **loose** in the spaces below.

I know everybody will be a grown-up some day. I just don't want to _____ my
$_1$

freedom to be myself. I'm kind of _____, you know, laid back. This isn't
$_2$

something that would make me _____ a job. Creativity requires an open
$_3$

and free mind. I think you have to be _____ to be creative. I will not
$_4$

_____ my self-discipline. I will be a self-disciplined grown-up.
$_5$

Write **lose** or **loose** in the spaces below. Remember, you **lose** something (one o). When something isn't tight, it's **loose** (two o's).

1. I'm going to _____ my mind!

2. How can a person _____ a mind?

3. What does "She has _____ lips" mean?

4. What does "He's as _____ as a goose" mean?

5. I sure don't want to _____ this.

6. Let _____!

7. The harness is too _____.

8. I like to wear _____ clothes.

9. She's afraid she'll _____ her money.

10. How did you _____ your shoes?

11. I was afraid I would _____ it.

12. What does it mean to be _____ with money?

Now write your own sentences using **lose** and **loose**.

1. _____

2. _____

Lost

Use **lost** to say that something is missing.

Example:
I **lost** my paycheck.

Loss

Use **loss** to describe the result of something missing.

Example:
Losing my paycheck was a huge **loss**.

Practice: Write **lost** or **loss** in the spaces below.

When I got home last Friday, I couldn't find my paycheck. I told my boss I

_____ it. She said she knew that was a huge _____ for me. She wrote me a
1   2

new check. She stopped payment on the _____ check so that the company
3

won't have a _____. From now on I'll be more careful. When something is
4

_____, you feel it for a long time.
5

Write **lost** or **loss** in the spaces below. Remember, use **loss** for the feeling you have when something is missing; use **lost** for the past tense of the verb *to lose*.

1. Her brother _____ his job.

2. My neighbor _____ a lot of weight.

3. Did you watch "The _____ Empire" on TV?

4. I have so many pennies that I _____ count.

5. A _____ mind is a real _____ .

6. My neighbor went to a weight _____ clinic.

7. Have you ever _____ anything?

8. He's suffering from the _____ of his friend.

9. I _____ my keys.

10. She _____ her car!

11. Have you ever had a big _____?

Now write your own sentences using **lost** and **loss**.

1. _____

2. _____

Make

Don't use **make** a party.

You **can** make something **for** the party: decorations, cake, invitations.

Use   **give** a party

      throw a party

      have a party

Practice: Write **make**, **give**, **throw**, or **have** in the spaces below.

Let's _____ a party. I'll _____ the invitations. You can _____ the
        1   2   3

food. We'll call this a practice party. This year we will _____ a graduation
                                                4

party. We will _____ an after-prom party. We will _____ an anniversary
               5   6

party for our parents. We need to _____ a lot of time for parties, don't we?
                                    7

Write **give**, **throw**, **have**, or **make** in the spaces below. Remember, people don't say "make a party" in standard English.

1. Let's _____ a party.

2. He wants to _____ cotton candy for the party.

3. A party is something we _____ for a special occasion.

4. They _____ a big party every spring.

5. Everyone is allowed to _____ themselves a party.

6. How many parties do you _____ each year?

7. Some people _____ parties and charge money to attend.

8. The parties that I _____ are free.

9. May I _____ cookies for the party?

10. She wants to _____ herself a birthday party.

Now write your own sentences using **give** and **make**.

1. _____

2. _____

Married With

Don't use married **with** your husband or wife.

Example of what __not__ to say:
She is getting **married** **with** Robert.

Married To

Use **married** **to** your husband or wife.

Examples:
She is getting **married** **to** her classmate.
Use *with* this way: She is **going** **with** her classmate.

Practice: Write **with** or **to** in the spaces below.

My cousin just told me she is getting married _____ Robert. I am getting married
₁

_____ my fiancé this year. We have all been best friends forever. We can have a
₂

double ceremony and share the costs. We can get married _____ flowers,
₃

candles, and live music. My cousin and I will get married _____ our fiancés in
₄

the wedding of our dreams.

Married With and To • Practice

Write **with** or **to** in the spaces below. Remember, in standard English people don't get married *with* a person.

1. Elizabeth is getting married _____ Tony.

2. I want to get married _____ 200 people in the church.

3. It seems like movie stars generally get married _____ each other.

4. Famous people get married _____ lots of cameras around.

5. She got married _____ her husband ten years ago.

6. Why does he want to get married _____ her?

7. He wants to get married _____ his whole family there.

8. We want to get married _____ each other in my parents' house.

9. He wants me to get married _____ him in the most romantic place.

10. Do you want to be married _____ me forever?

Now write your own sentences using **married with** and **married to**.

1. _____

2. _____

Might Can

Don't use **might can**.

*Example of what **not** to say:*
I **might can** come over.

Maybe

Use **may be able to** or **maybe**.

Example:
I **may be able to** come over.

Example:
Maybe I can come over.

Practice: Write **may be able to** or **maybe** in the spaces below.

I _____ sing at the school dance. _____ I
  1   2

can find a way to make the dance committee choose me. Let's see. I

_____ make a tape for them. Or I _____
3   4

persuade them to come to church and hear me. Or _____
                                                                     5

I could serenade them at school.

Write **may be able to** or **maybe** in the spaces below. Remember not to use *might can*.

1. I _____ study guitar.

2. I _____ come.

3. We _____ return it tomorrow.

4. I believe I _____ do that!

5. _____ I can do it.

6. _____ I can go Saturday night.

7. _____ I can.

8. He _____ make it on time.

9. I _____ fly.

10. _____ I can eat the whole pizza.

11. _____ he can, and _____ he can't.

Now write your own sentences using **maybe** and **may be able to**.

1. _____

2. _____

Mines

Don't use **mines** if you mean something belongs to you.

Example of what __not__ to say:
These books are **mines**.

Mine

Use **mine** (no *s*) if something belongs to you.

Example:
These books are **mine**, too.

Or use **mines** when you mean more than one mine.

Example:
She has five gold **mines**.

Practice: Write **mines** or **mine** in the spaces below.

I own 1,000 diamond _____, 500 platinum _____, and 250 gold
                           1   2

_____. Each one is all _____! I found them, dug them, and mined them.
3   4

It's fun. This diamond is _____. This gold is _____. I can sell them, but
                                  5   6

I'd rather share them. We always say to each other, "What's _____ is yours."
                                                                           7

Write **mines** or **mine** in the spaces below. Remember, the possessive **mine** doesn't have an *s*.

1. Princess Diana worked to get rid of land _____.

2. Have you heard of the South African diamond _____?

3. Are there coal _____ in every state?

4. This is _____.

5. Those earrings are _____.

6. That one is _____.

7. I think the _____ are over there.

8. The hair clips are _____.

9. Hey! That's _____.

10. "_____ is the best," he said playfully.

Now write your own sentences using **mines** and **mine**.

1. _____

2. _____

Know

Use **know** when you mean you understand something or have the facts.

Example:
I **know** everything about porpoises.

No

Use **no** if you mean a refusal, a denial, or a lack of something.

Example:
No, you cannot eat the porpoise.

Practice: Write **no** or **know** in the spaces below.

That's _____ porpoise. That's a whale! I _____ how to tell a porpoise from a
    1   2

whale! A porpoise has _____ blow-hole; a whale does. I _____ that they
                            3   4

have different shapes, but I don't _____ how to describe them. I _____ that
                                         5   6

they eat the same thing. But that is _____ help, is it? Trust me. There is
                                           7

_____ porpoise as big as what you are seeing—and there's _____ purpose
8   9

at all in insisting that there is.

Write **no** or **know** in the spaces below. Use **no** if you mean *n-o*; use **know** if you mean knowledge.

1. You _____ I said _____.

2. _____, I don't.

3. I _____ the way.

4. _____ you don't, Hector.

5. I _____ I read that somewhere.

6. I _____ nothing about that.

7. I have _____ facts.

8. I don't _____ how to dance.

9. How does the refrigerator _____ when to turn on?

10. Do you _____ who's coming to dinner?

11. He wants to _____ how to do that.

12. She doesn't _____ the way.

Now write your own sentences using **no** and **know**.

1. _____

2. _____

Not with Nothing and Anything

Not with Nothing

Don't use **not** with **nothing**.

Example of what __not__ to say:
There's **not** **nothing** here I want.

Not with Anything

Use **not** with **anything**.

Example:
There's **not anything** here that I want.

Or use **nothing** alone.

Example:
There's **nothing** here that I want.

Practice: Write **nothing** or **anything** in the spaces below.

I don't have _____ to complain about. I have my friends, a pretty good
1

job, and a great sound system. In the future, I will have more. Right now, there

isn't _____ missing in my life. People in the movies have more than I
2

do, but that's the movies. I don't need _____. I don't miss
3

_____, and there is _____ that I can't do if I try.
4   5

Not with Nothing and Anything • Practice

Write **nothing** or **anything** in the spaces below. Remember, don't use two negative words (**not** and **nothing**) together.

1. I don't have _____ to do for an hour.

2. There isn't _____ on my calendar for tomorrow.

3. That's not a big bump, but I wouldn't say it's _____.

4. I can't do _____ without my little brother.

5. She won't do _____ about it.

6. Great! There's not _____ left to do.

7. Great! There's _____ left to do.

8. There isn't _____ to eat in the refrigerator.

9. I don't think _____ is wrong with the engine.

10. I'm not taking _____ with me except a pencil.

11. Are you sure there's _____ I can do for you?

Now write your own sentences using **anything** and **nothing**.

1. _____

2. _____

Now

Don't use I **now** you.

Know

Use I **know** you.

Example:
Now I **know** who you are!

Practice: Write **now** or **know** in the spaces below.

Right _____, I _____ what I want. But I _____ that next year I might be
1 2 3

different. Next year, I might say, "_____ I really _____ what I want!" My
4 5

dad tells me not to make any big decisions right _____. He says he changed
6

and so will I. I _____ he is right. But isn't what I want _____ important? He
7 8

says be careful what I do _____ so I can have good choices later.
9

Write **now** or **know** in the spaces below. Remember, **now** with an *n* means immediately. **Know** with a *k* means that you understand or recognize something.

1. I _____ better _____.

2. _____ begins with a *k*. _____ doesn't.

3. _____ I _____ how to get here.

4. I _____ some things better than I _____ others.

5. How will I _____?

6. Well, what do you _____?

7. I want to _____ everything about music.

8. Is _____ a good time to do it?

9. I _____ what I want.

10. I want it _____.

11. I _____ I can do it.

12. I _____ you can, too.

Now write your own sentences using **now** and **know**.

1. _____

2. _____

Our

Use **our** if you mean *belonging to us*.

Example:
Our house is at the end of the block.

Are

Use **are** for the verb *to be*: I **am**; you, we, and they **are**; he, she, and it **is**.

Example:
We **are** going home first.

Practice: Write **our** or **are** in the spaces below.

They _____ going to meet at _____ house. Then we _____ all going to the play
     1   2   3

at _____ school. _____ you coming too, Auntie? You _____ _____ favorite aunt.
   4   5   6   7

Oh, I know, you _____ going to say that you _____ _____ only aunt.
                 8   9   10

If we had 40 aunts, you would still win _____ vote. _____ you persuaded,
                               11   12

Auntie? _____ you coming to our school play?
     13

Write **our** and **are** in the spaces below. Remember, use **our** when you mean yours and mine; use **are** when you need the verb.

1. They _____ _____best customers.

2. Sometimes we _____ _____ own worst enemies.

3. _____ you here?

4. All _____ friends _____ here.

5. _____ kids _____ all boys.

6. _____ you sure this is _____ car?

7. _____ best chance is _____ confidence.

8. _____ you with me, or _____ you not?

9. We _____ happy.

10. _____ friends _____ happy.

11. _____ time has come.

12. We _____ ready!

Now write your own sentences using **our** and **are**.

1. _____

2. _____

Pass By

Don't use **pass by** to say you'll be there.

Stop By

Use **stop by**, **come over**, or **show up**.

Examples:
They'll **stop by** for a while.
I'll **come over** to your house.
He'll **show up** at the end of the party.

Practice: Write **stop by**, **come over**, **show up**, or **pass by** in the spaces below.

You said you would _____ to my house. I waited for you, but you
                                    1

honked and kept driving. Then, you told me you would _____ at 8:00. At
     2

8:30 you honked, and I saw you _____. I wish you would actually come
     3

inside and visit me. Why don't you _____ and stay a while?
     4

Write **pass by**, **stop by**, **come over**, or **show up** in the spaces below.

1. _____ to my house for a little while.

2. Of course I'll _____ at my own graduation!

3. Mom's friend will _____ to our house this weekend.

4. Do you have time to _____ for dessert?

5. I don't want to stop. I just want to _____.

6. How often does he _____ to watch TV?

7. You _____ my house on the way to her house.

8. If there isn't any mail, the mailman will just _____ our house.

9. I'll _____ about 6:00.

10. They'll _____ to talk about it this afternoon.

11. He wants to _____ on his way to school.

Now write your own sentences using **pass by** and any other choice from the list above.

1. _____

2. _____

Past

Use **past** when you mean a former time.

Example:
In the **past**, I was very shy.

Passed

Use **passed** when you mean an action that is completed.

Example:
I **passed** a post office on my way here.

Practice: Write **past** or **passed** in the spaces below.

Being shy is entirely in my _____. It wasn't fun for me. I _____ up a
                              1   2

lot of good times. I probably _____ up good friendships, too. Many people
                              3

are shy until someone says, "You don't have to be afraid." I applied for college,

and I _____ the entrance exams. I applied for a job, and I _____ the
      4   5

interview. I may have a shy _____, but I have a confident future.
                            6

Write **past** or **passed** in the spaces below. Use **past** when you're talking about time; use **passed** when you are talking about an action.

1. The bus just _____ us by!

2. They _____ the cookies around, and when they got to me, there were none left.

3. He _____ his hat, and people put money in it.

4. I thought she was _____ that.

5. He had a really hard _____.

6. I'm _____ president of my club.

7. Everyone in class _____ the test.

8. I have used that brand in the _____.

9. Aw, that's in the _____. Forget it.

10. Have you _____ out the prizes yet?

11. I _____ up a great opportunity!

Now write your own sentences using **past** and **passed**.

1. _____

2. _____

Right Now

Don't use **right now** if you mean something has just happened.

*Example of what **not** to say:*
She left **right now**!

Already

Use **already** when something has just happened.

Example:
She **already** left!

Practice: Write **right now** or **already** in the spaces below.

My mom said, "Turn off the TV _____." I told her that I

1

_____ had. She asked me when I was going to start my homework. I

2

said that I _____ had. She said, "What?" I said, "Okay, I'm starting

3

_____." I asked her when she was going to work. She said,

4

"_____!" and that my homework should be done by the time she

5

returned.

Write **right now** or **already** in the spaces below. Remember, **right now** means at this very moment; **already** means you have started or finished something.

1. I am _____ finished.

2. I am finishing _____.

3. She's coming here _____.

4. He has _____ left.

5. He left _____.

6. Later. I am tired _____.

7. We just started, and she's tired _____.

8. I got a job _____.

9. The dog is housebroken _____.

10. It's 2:00. I have to go home _____.

Now write your own sentences using **right now** and **already**.

1. _____

2. _____

Sense

Use **sense** if you mean feeling or perceiving.

Example:
I can **sense** that he's been here.

Since

Use **since** to show a time relationship, or as because.

Examples:
He's been here **since** the last time we looked.
Since he's just a pup, he probably doesn't know he's lost.

Practice: Write **sense** or **since** in the spaces below.

I've wanted a dog _____ I was a little kid. My dad and mom said it didn't

1

make _____ to keep a dog in a small apartment. Now we have a house and a

2

yard. "It's just common _____," my dad said, "to have a puppy in that

3

yard!" I was very happy. Now, _____ I didn't have the _____ to lock the

4   5

gate, I'm out looking for my puppy.

Write **sense** or **since** in the spaces below. Remember, **sense** refers to something you feel; **since** refers to time, or can be used as *because*.

1. How's your _____ of smell?

2. Does it make _____ to go home first?

3. I haven't been to the park _____ last summer.

4. This should please your _____ of taste.

5. I can _____ trouble even before I see it.

6. _____ you're here, let's have a little chat.

7. Have you been to the house _____ it was remodeled?

8. Ever _____ the rain, the grass has remained green!

9. _____ we're twins, we always know what each other is thinking.

10. Which animal has the best _____ of smell?

11. You say nothing's wrong, but I _____ that something is.

12. He can do no wrong _____ he's the king.

Now write your own sentences using **sense** and **since**.

1. _____

2. _____

Stayed

Use **stayed** when you were somewhere for a while.

Example:
I **stayed** at my aunt's house.

Stood

Use **stood** when you mean the past of *to stand*.

Example:
The bus was full, so I **stood** all the way.

Practice: Write **stayed** or **stood** in the spaces below.

I went to my nephew's birthday party. Everyone there was little, and I just

_____ around. Then I went to the kitchen. I _____ there for a while.
1   2

Then I went into the backyard. There were no chairs, so I _____ in the
                                                                          3

yard with nothing to do. Finally, someone my age came. I felt better, so I

_____ a long time.
4

Write **stayed** or **stood** in the spaces below. Use **stayed** when you want the past of *to stay*; use **stood** when you want the past of *to stand*.

1. I _____ in Mexico with my uncle.

2. I _____ in line for four hours.

3. He _____ up for his beliefs.

4. He _____ up too late watching TV.

5. She _____ in the car while he turned in his homework.

6. He _____ up to them.

7. We _____ in school so we could go to college.

8. She _____ loyal to him for many years.

9. How long has he _____ at your house?

10. He _____ on one leg for four hours.

11. She _____ it up in the corner.

12. He was happy he _____ with it until he learned it.

Now write your own sentences using **stayed** and **stood**.

1. _____

2. _____

Stepped Out

Don't use **stepped out** if someone has gone home for the day.

Left

Use **left for the day** or **isn't in**.

Example:
Sorry. She has **left for the day**.

Practice: Write **left**, **isn't in**, or **stepped out** in the spaces below.

Customer Service. May I help you? I'm sorry, Mrs. Gale has

_____ for the day. Mr. Vasquez is here, but he
1

_____ for a few minutes. Miss Chung
2

_____ at the moment, but I expect her later this
3

afternoon. Would you like to leave a message?

Write **stepped out**, **left**, or **isn't in** in the spaces below.

1. I know he's here. He must have _____ for a short time.

2. They all _____ for the meeting.

3. The entire office _____ for the day.

4. She _____ today.

5. The bank manager _____. May I help you?

6. Marla _____ for a minute.

7. He _____ the office this week.

8. My mother just _____ for work.

9. Charles already _____ for the game.

10. Your hair stylist _____ until next Saturday.

Now write your own sentences using **stepped out** and **left**.

1. _____

2. _____

Suppose and Supposed To

Suppose

Use **suppose** if something could be true.

Example:
I **suppose** it's possible.

Supposed To

Use **supposed to** if something is expected.

Example:
I am **supposed to** go to the library.

Practice: Write **suppose** or **supposed to** in the spaces below.

The dance is tomorrow night. I ordered my dress from a catalog. It is

_____ arrive today. I _____ it could come tomorrow.
1   2

What am I _____ wear if the dress doesn't come?
                      3

I _____ I could wear what I wore last year. But this dance is
    4

_____ be very special. Oh, well, I _____ I will have a
5   6

good time no matter what I wear.

Suppose and Supposed To • Practice

Write **suppose** or **supposed to** in the spaces below. Use **suppose** if something is possible; use **supposed to** if something is expected.

1. I _____ I should start dinner.

2. Do you _____ it's true?

3. We're _____ know.

4. I'm _____ visit my uncle tomorrow.

5. _____ the sky falls!

6. Whom do you _____ that is?

7. Am I _____ know?

8. We're _____ dress up.

9. She's _____ have her baby next week.

10. It's _____ rain tonight.

11. I _____ I'll stay in.

Now write your own sentences using **suppose** and **supposed to**.

1. _____

2. _____

Their, There, and They're

Their

Use **their** when something belongs to something or someone.

Example:
We went to **their** house.

There

Use **there** to show where something is.

Example:
It's over **there**!

They're

Use **they're** when you mean *they are*.

Example:
They're bad!

Practice: Write **their**, **there**, or **they're** in the spaces below.

I go to _____ house frequently. I think _____ very nice. When I get
___1___   ___2___

_____, they always invite me to eat lunch. I feel that _____
___3___   ___4___

very kind and also that _____ food is very good. I think I'll go back
                       ___5___

_____ many times.
___6___

Their, There, and They're • Practice

Write **their**, **there**, or **they're** in the spaces below. Use **their** to show possession, **there** to show location, and **they're** for the contraction of *they are*.

1. I went to _____ house yesterday.

2. _____ okay.

3. It's over _____.

4. _____ money is red, green, and yellow.

5. He thinks _____ food is delicious.

6. _____ responsible for _____ actions.

7. _____ she goes, running as usual!

8. _____ mother is waiting for them.

9. _____ is no place like home.

10. _____ way cool.

Now write your own sentences using **their**, **there**, and **they're**.

1. _____

2. _____

3. _____

Them

Don't use **them** if a person, place, or thing follows the word.

*Example of what **not** to say:*
Give me some of **them** cookies.

Those

Use **those**.

Example:
Give me some of **those** cookies.

Or use **them** alone.

Example:
Give me some of **them**.

Practice: Write **them** or **those** in the spaces below.

When strawberries are in season, you can buy more of _____ for less

1

money. _____ fruit-stand strawberries taste better than anything! Once I

2

gave some to my grandmother. She still remembers. She says, "Oh, _____

3

strawberries!" Today, I will buy her a pound of _____. Then, I will wait

4

and see if she says, "Oh, _____ strawberries!"

5

Write **them** or **those** in the spaces below. Remember, don't use **them** if a noun (a person, place, or thing) follows the word; use **those**.

1. _____ kids are very smart.

2. Hang around with _____, why don't you?

3. I like _____ lamps more than I like _____ lamps.

4. Do you have more of _____ roses?

5. What are _____ workers doing?

6. Let's go ask _____.

7. Take these, but not _____.

8. _____ are classy "shades"!

9. Ask _____.

10. _____ people don't know.

11. Love _____ burgers!

12. Hang up _____ clothes!

Now write your own sentences using **them** and **those**.

1. _____

2. _____

Then

Use **then** if you are talking about time.

Example:
Let's get ice cream first and **then** the donuts!

Than

Use **than** when you are comparing two words.

Example:
I like chocolate more **than** vanilla.

Practice: Write **then** or **than** in the spaces below.

My family likes to watch the news on television. I like cable news more

_____ network news. So we watch the network news. _____ we watch
1   2

the cable news. My brother says the newspaper is better _____ television.
3

He watches network news. _____ he watches the cable news. _____ he
4   5

reads the newspaper. My father says my brother knows more news _____
6

the rest of us.

Write **then** or **than** in the spaces below. Use **then** to talk about what happened next; use **than** to compare or contrast.

1. I ate. _____ I went to bed.

2. I'm hungrier _____ you are.

3. He's taller _____ she is.

4. _____ we went shopping.

5. They are richer _____ we are.

6. _____ they moved to Texas.

7. I am nicer _____ you are.

8. I am prettier _____ you are.

9. He likes tamales more _____ hamburgers.

10. Let's go home, do your homework, _____ watch TV.

11. She is a better teacher _____ she was last year.

Now write your own sentences using **then** and **than**.

1. _____

2. _____

Thought

Use **thought** when you mean thinking; the past of *to think*.

Example:
I **thought** I was too young to be wise.

Though

Use **though** to say, "in spite of the fact that . . ."

Example:
I'm wise, **though** I'm young.

Practice: Write **thought** or **though** in the spaces below.

My teacher says I am wise, _____ I don't always show it. I _____

1   2

about that. Being athletic shows, even _____ you're not playing. Being

3

wise is an inside thing. I _____, "How does being wise show?"

4

I _____ the dictionary could tell me. *Wise* means having good judgment.

5

It means knowing what is true and what is a lie. Now, there's a _____!

6

Thought and Though • Practice

Write **thought** or **though** in the spaces below. Remember, use **thought** (with a *t*) when you mean the past of *to think*.

1. I _____ you liked me.

2. To tell you the truth, I haven't _____ about it.

3. She _____ she wanted to be a nurse.

4. I _____ you were going with us.

5. She's going to perform, even _____ she is hoarse tonight.

6. Even _____ he's rich, he wants more money.

7. We _____ you'd be happy.

8. He paints continuously, _____ he hasn't sold any paintings.

9. I told her I'd come, even _____ I don't want to.

10. The present, past, and past participles are think, _____, and _____.

Now write your own sentences using **thought** and **though**.

1. _____

2. _____

Threw

Use **threw** to say the past of *to throw*.

Example:
He **threw** the ball.

Through

Use **through** when you mean *all the way*.

Example:
She ran **through** the crowd to catch it.

Practice: Write **threw** or **through** in the spaces below.

I'm _____ going to school. I _____ my books away. I _____ my
        1   2   3

backpack away. I'm _____ caring. I'm _____ trying. Maybe I should think
                          4   5

this _____. I'll ask for a transfer. When it comes _____, I'll go to a
        6   7

different school. Where did I throw my backpack? Oh, no! I have to go _____
                                                                              8

the dumpster!

Threw and Through • Practice

Write **threw** or **through** in the spaces below. Remember, use **threw** when you mean the past of *to throw*; use **through** the rest of the time.

1. My job fell _____.

2. I'm sorry I _____ the ball _____ your window.

3. He _____ himself into his work.

4. When my transfer comes _____, I'm moving to Atlanta.

5. Look who just walked _____ the door!

6. I'm looking forward to being _____ with all this.

7. He _____ up.

8. He _____ the javelin.

9. She _____ the dice.

10. Come _____ the lobby and up the stairs.

11. He _____ out all his old clothes.

12. Did he get _____, or was the line busy?

Now write your own sentences using **threw** and **through**.

1. _____

2. _____

Too

Use **too** when you mean *also*.

Examples:

I want **to** go, **too**.

You, **too**, have been selected **to** go.

He is happy, she is happy, and I am happy, **too**.

Practice: Write **to** or **too** in the spaces below.

I want ____ go ____ Disney World. My dad wants ____ see Washington, D.C.
     1   2   3

Disney World is fun. Washington, D.C., is serious. I will probably have ____ learn
                                                                    4

things there. Dad says D.C. has fun things, ____. He thinks museums are fun. I
                                               5

will suggest a compromise. First, we go ____ Disney World. If there is enough
                                             6

time, we will visit D.C. ____.
                           7

Write **to** or **too** in the spaces below. Remember, use **too** when you mean *also*; use **to** the rest of the time.

1. I want to go, _____.

2. Let's all go _____ the park.

3. We are friends _____ the end!

4. Am I your friend, _____?

5. I have a sore throat, _____.

6. Do you want _____ go _____ the clinic?

7. This room is empty, _____.

8. Let's go _____ the empty room.

9. I have a dog, _____.

10. She lives here, _____.

11. This one is pretty, _____.

12. He, _____, is a high-school student.

Now write your own sentences using **to** and **too**.

1. _____

2. _____

To and Too (as in *more than necessary*)

Too

Use **too** when something is more than necessary.

Examples:

It's **too** cold in here.

The soup is **too** hot to handle.

He's **too** handsome for his own good.

Practice: Write **to** or **too** in the spaces below.

I don't like _____ go _____ the dentist. We have _____ wait _____ long _____ get in.

1   2   3   4   5

There are _____ many people waiting. It is _____ crowded, _____ noisy, and _____

6   7   8   9

hot. Finally, when I get in _____ see her, everything is fine. She is nice. She tells

10

me _____ floss my teeth. I say it hurts _____ much. She says it won't hurt if I do it

11   12

every day. She asks me _____ try. I say I want _____ go home and start right now.

13   14

She laughs.

Write **to** or **too** in the spaces below. Remember, use **too** when you're saying that something is more than necessary. Otherwise, use **to**.

1. It's _____ late to go _____ the store.

2. You are _____ young _____ go alone.

3. As the saying goes, "_____ many cooks spoil the soup."

4. It's _____ hot in here.

5. This test is _____ long _____ finish in an hour.

6. I'll go _____ the store, even if it is _____ late _____ go out.

7. This bus goes _____ the beach, but it takes _____ long.

8. He wrote _____ me from Ecuador.

9. I'm _____ tall.

10. I'm _____ short.

11. I'm _____ tired.

12. I'm _____ smart _____ get this wrong.

Now write your own sentences using **to** and **too**.

1. _____

2. _____

Too

Use **too** if you mean something is more than it should be.

Example:
It is noisy because we live **too** close to the airport.

Very

Use **very** to emphasize something.

Example:
We live **very** close to the airport.

Practice: Write **too** or **very** in the spaces below.

I want to go to the beach on Saturday _____ much. My dad said it is
₁

_____ far for me to drive by myself. I asked my cousin to go with me. My
₂

cousin is _____ young to drive, but she is _____ responsible. My dad said
₃ ₄

we can take the car if we are _____ careful and don't drive _____ fast. So
₅ ₆

I am going to the beach, and I am _____ happy.
₇

Write **too** or **very** in the spaces below. Remember, use **too** when something is more than it should be; use **very** when you just mean it's a lot.

1. He worships her. I think he likes her way _____ much.

2. He respects her. I think he likes her _____ much.

3. I think it's _____ cold for comfort.

4. It's _____ cold in here. It feels good!

5. The movie was _____ complicated. I'm going to see it again.

6. The movie was _____ complicated. That's why it didn't win.

7. He is _____ good to me. I appreciate him.

8. He is _____ good. She's going to take advantage of him.

9. He's nice to me. I like that _____ much.

10. It's _____ hot today. I don't like this weather.

11. She is _____ smart.

12. You are doing _____ much for me.

Now write your own sentences using **too** and **very**.

1. _____

2. _____

Until

Don't use **<u>until</u>** without **<u>not</u>** when you're saying what won't happen by a certain time.

Example of what <u>not</u> to say:
We're eating **<u>until</u>** 8:00 tonight.

Use **<u>until</u>** with **<u>not</u>** when you're saying what won't happen by a certain time.

Example:
We will not eat dinner **<u>until</u>** 8:00.

Practice: Write **<u>can't</u>**, **<u>won't</u>**, or **<u>not</u>** with **<u>until</u>** in the spaces below.

I invited my friends to watch a movie on HBO. I said, "It starts at 7:00." They

said, "Okay." Then, one by one, they called and said, "I _____ be there until

1

8:00." "I _____ be there until 8:30." "I _____ come until 8:45." So

2   3

they're _____ coming until the movie is almost over! This will be a very

4

strange TV party.

Until • Practice

Write **can't**, **won't**, or **not** in the spaces below. Remember, use **not** *with* **until** when you're saying something won't happen by a certain time.

1. She's _____ returning to work until Monday.

2. They _____ finish until midnight.

3. Summer _____ begin until late in June.

4. He _____ get here until Saturday.

5. The bank _____ open until security comes.

6. I _____ call you until my phone is fixed.

7. He's _____ playing soccer until his ankle heals.

8. Grandma _____ go out until she puts her teeth in!

9. She's _____ going until next Tuesday.

10. The package is _____ coming until after Christmas.

11. The lights _____ come on until after dark.

12. Our cat _____ come home until he's ready.

Now write your own sentence using **until** with **can't**, **won't**, or **not**.

1. _____

Vacations

Use **vacations** when you mean more than one vacation.

Example:
I am taking two one-week **vacations** this year.

Vacation

Use **vacation** when you mean one vacation, even if it's more than one day.

Example:
She is on **vacation** from December 12 to January 1.

Practice: Write **vacations** or **vacation** in the spaces below.

Our family likes to go on _____. Our favorite _____ was

1
2

the time we went to Yosemite. My dad gets five days for each of his

_____, and he gets two _____ a year. As we are
3
4

_____-lovers, it's not enough.
5

Write **vacations** or **vacation** in the spaces below. Remember, in standard English, a vacation has no *s*.

1. Do you get a _____ this year?

2. Does everyone get a _____ at this company?

3. One more week until my _____!

4. How many _____ do you get at this school?

5. My mom has never had a paid _____.

6. Were you on _____?

7. The whole school is on _____ this week.

8. I wish I were on _____ right now.

9. What do you do with the iguana during summer _____?

Now write your own sentences using **vacations** and **vacation**.

1. _____

2. _____

We're

Use **we're** if you mean *we are*.

Example:
We're going!

Were

Use **were** if you mean the past of the verb *to be*.

Example:
Where **were** you last night?

Practice: Write **we're** or **were** in the spaces below.

_____ two people who want to go to college. We _____ sure of this when

1   2

we _____ in elementary school. Some friends say _____ crazy. Some teachers

    3   4

have said _____ not ready. We know _____ able to do anything if we work

               5   6

hard. _____ working hard. In a few years, people will say, "They were right,"

       7

because guess what? _____ already accepted at a community college.

                            8

We're and Were • Practice

Write **we're** or **were** in the spaces below. Remember, use **we're** when you mean *we are*; use **were** when you mean the past of the verb *to be*.

1. _____ you at the movies?

2. _____ very happy with your work.

3. We'll tell you where _____ going later.

4. _____ you in Europe or Mexico for your vacation?

5. Where _____ going is going to be a surprise.

6. They're swimmers; _____ football players.

7. You're okay. _____ so-so.

8. They _____ 15 last year.

9. _____ tired of wondering about where you _____.

10. _____ relieved that this problem is solved.

11. Where _____ you planning to celebrate?

Now write your own sentences using **we're** and **were**.

1. _____

2. _____

When

Use **when** (with an *h*) if you mean time.

Example:
We'll go **when** your dad gets home.

Went

Use **went** (with a *t*) if you mean the past of *go*.

Example:
When Dad got home, we **went** to the video store.

Practice: Write **when** or **went** in the spaces below.

Person 1:   _____ did you guys rent the video?
             1

Person 2:   Today. We _____ with Dad. We'll watch it _____ you get here.
                       2   3

Person 1:   Cool. _____ I _____ to the video store, it was checked out.
                   4   5

Person 2:   We were lucky. It had just been returned _____ we walked in.
                                                      6

Person 1:   Outstanding. _____ I want something, I'll take your dad with me!
                          7

When and Went • Practice

Write **when** or **went** in the spaces below. Remember, w<u>h</u>en has an *h*; wen<u>t</u> has a *t*.

1. _____ did you last see him?

2. You want it _____?

3. I _____ alone _____ I learned she couldn't come.

4. I like school _____ I'm doing well.

5. I _____ along with them.

6. They really _____ to town!

7. Do you know _____ he'll return?

8. My friend eats popsicles _____ she's sick.

9. She _____ to the library instead.

10. The parade will begin _____ the horses are ready.

11. Who _____ _____ you did?

12. _____ he _____ away, he put his things in storage.

Now write your own sentences using **when** and **went**.

1. _____

2. _____

Whether

Use **whether** when you wonder if something is so.

Example:
Do you know **whether** they're open today?

Weather

Use **weather** if you mean the climate.

Example:
What's the **weather** like in Portugal?

Practice: Write **whether** or **weather** in the spaces below.

Last year my brother went to a summer camp on a farm. I don't know

_____ he liked everything. I don't know _____ he made friends, or
1   2

_____ the food was any good, but he said that the _____ was
3   4

nice—sunny but not too hot. He learned some new words there, too. A sow is a

female pig. A ewe is a female lamb. A wether is a castrated lamb.

Whether and Weather • Practice

Write **whether** or **weather** in the spaces below. Remember, **whether** means *if*, and **weather** means *climate*.

1. Everyone is talking about the _____ this year.

2. I don't know _____ I'm hot or cold.

3. He hasn't said _____ he's going.

4. I like the _____ at the beach.

5. _____ he likes it or not, I'm buying it.

6. The story didn't say _____ the main character was good.

7. Do you know _____ they're friendly there?

8. The _____ where they're from is very humid.

9. I'm not used to this _____.

10. Geography helps explain why the _____ is different in different places.

11. I want to be a _____ person on TV.

Now write your own sentences using **whether** and **weather**.

1. _____

2. _____

Who's and Whose

Who's

Use **who's** if you mean *who is*.

Example:
Who's that?

Whose

Use **whose** when something belongs to someone.

Example:
Whose cap is that?

Practice: Write **who's** or **whose** in the spaces below.

I taught my dog to play hide-and-seek. He hides under a blanket. I say,

"_____ that? _____ dog is that?" He runs into a big paper bag.
　　1　　　　　　　　　　　2

He waits for me to say, "_____ in that bag?" Then he hides under my
　　　　　　　　　　　　　　3

jacket and attacks the sleeve. "_____ jacket was that?" I ask. Then I
　　　　　　　　　　　　　　　　　4

wonder. _____ game is this anyway, and _____ making the rules?
　　　　　5　　　　　　　　　　　　　　　　6

Write **who's** or **whose** in the spaces below. Remember, use **who's** when you mean *who is*; use **whose** when you're referring to someone's possession

1. _____ going to pay the check?

2. I don't know _____ it is.

3. Do you know _____ birthday it is?

4. _____ life is it, anyway?

5. _____ this?

6. I don't care _____ boyfriend he is.

7. _____ going to take me home?

8. She gave the book to the student _____ going to read it.

9. _____ that?

10. This is for the woman _____ husband loves surprises.

11. _____ dollar is this?

Now write your own sentences using **who's** and **whose**.

1. _____

2. _____

Worse

Use **worse** if something is less good than something else.

Example:
This movie is **worse** than you said it would be.

Worst

Use **worst** if something is as bad as it gets.

Example:
This is the **worst** movie I have ever seen.

Practice: Write **worse** or **worst** in the spaces below.

I don't know which is _____—a bad movie or no movie at all. However,
1

the _____ movie I have seen wasn't actually boring. It had a lot of action.
2

The story went from bad to _____ and then to the absolute _____.
3 4

I admit, however, that my problem could have been the popcorn. It was bad. It

was _____ than chewing cotton balls.
5

Write **worse** or **worst** in the spaces below. Remember, use **worse** if something is less good than something else; use **worst** if it's as bad as it gets.

1. Which is _____—doing homework or having no homework to turn in?

2. My _____ day was when I got lost.

3. I'm afraid she's getting _____, not better.

4. This year's flood was the _____ in 50 years.

5. In many cities, air quality is getting better, not _____.

6. Let's get married "for better or for _____."

7. I think your fears are _____ than mine.

8. Tell us about your _____ nightmare!

9. He's very nice, but he's the _____ cook in the world!

10. My bedroom is in the _____ condition it's ever been in.

11. What's the _____-tasting food in the world?

Now write your own sentences using **worse** and **worst**.

1. _____

2. _____

You're

Use **you're** when you mean *you are*.

Example:
You're astonishing!

Your

Use **your** when you mean something belongs to someone.

Example:
I think **your** behavior is amazing!

Practice: Write **you're** or **your** in the spaces below.

_____ clever! And I know this is just part of _____ personality.
  1   2

_____ also thoughtful, careful, and amusing. Plus, I like _____ hair
  3   4

and _____ eyes. I would say _____ pretty well put together!
      5   6

Write **you're** or **your** in the spaces below. Remember, use **you're** when you mean *you are*; use **your** when you are referring to someone's possession.

1. I like _____ haircut.

2., He thinks _____ a nice girl.

3. _____ Catholic?

4. Where is _____ sweater?

5. _____ a smart student.

6. Do you have _____ lunch money?

7. I think _____ sunburned.

8. _____ in debt to me!

9. I like _____ style.

10. _____ to be here at 8:00 A.M.

11. People sometimes say, "_____ future is up to you."

Now write your own sentences using **you're** and **your**.

1. _____

2. _____

Circle the correct word in the sentences below.

1. My shoelace was (loose / lose), and I tripped!

2. These days there are (fewer / less) TV programs that I like.

3. (He's / His) going to the basketball game tonight.

4. I'm (gonna / going to) have some fun!

5. They shop downtown (for / because) prices are better there.

6. Let's eat something (else / more) instead.

7. They don't have (any / none) of that.

8. The law says we (don't have to / must not) bring weapons to school.

9. Please (close / turn off) the lights when you leave.

10. I'm afraid I'll (break / brake) it.

11. He's going to (tell / ask) if he can borrow it.

12. I found everything (except / accept) my English book.

13. Will you (borrow / loan) me the money?

14. He has (nothing / anything) to do.

15. Yesterday, my mom (loss / lost) her wallet.

16. We're going to (make / give) a party for her.

17. Those earrings are (mines / mine)!

18. Come over to (are / our) house on Saturday.

19. I've been lonely (since / sense) you've been gone.

20. (There / They're / Their) all going together.

21. I think (were / we're) lost.

22. The storm is getting (worst / worse).

23. I (though / thought) for sure I would fail, but I didn't!

24. The time (past / passed) very fast, didn't it?

25. When will we (now / know)?

26. He doesn't want to get married (with / to) her.

27. It doesn't have (any / no) tires.

28 They're (barely / just) burned.

29. The mall stores don't have (anything / nothing) I like.

30. (Can / May) I have more cookies?

31. Our baby cries (every time / all the time).

32. I (fell / feel) like going for a walk.

33. I'll take the umbrella (for / so) we won't get wet.

34. It seems like the weeds are (anywhere / everywhere).

35. I'm going to buy more of (them / those) paper towels.

36. He's on (vacations / vacation).

37. I don't want (none / any) of these.

38. She (don't / doesn't) like to swim.

39. They won't buy (either / neither) one.

40. I think I'll have something (more / else) this time.

41. This park doesn't charge (no / any) entrance fee.

42. They will announce the (because / cause) of the fire.

43. Do you (got / have) any milk?

44. How many (lifes / lives) does a cat have?

45. Don't (loose / lose) your keys!

46. I'm (suppose / supposed) to be home at 9:00.

47. I think this is (they're / there / their) house.

48. That was in the (past / passed).

49. That came (very / too) close for comfort.

50. I don't (no / know) where that came from!

51. There isn't (nothing / anything) I can do about it.

52. They've gone (too / to) the movies.

53. She (through / threw) a curve ball and won the game.

54. I don't know (weather / whether) to go or stay.

55. They don't (no / know) for sure.

56. I hope we have (fewer / less) heat this summer.

57. They left (to / for) the mountains.

58. We don't have (any / no) oranges.

59. Will you (borrow / loan) me your sweater, Mom?

60. I (barely / just) turned on the TV a minute ago.

61. The rule is that I (don't have to / must not) drink alcohol.

62. It (doesn't / don't) make sense.

63. I (break / brake) for small children.

64. I'm sure I (may / can) come over later.

65. We don't have (nothing / anything) to complain about.

66. (Either / Neither) of us has any money!

67. Ooops! I should (of / have) looked where I was going.

68. (Every time / All the time) I see him, my heart beats.

69. I like this one better (then / than) that one.

70. (Your / You're) more than halfway through!

71. How's the (whether / weather) up there?

72. We get two weeks of (vacations / vacation) at my job.

73. (Went / When) shall we go?

74. We should go (know / now).

75. Watch (you're / your) head!

76. She has a lot of common (since / sense).

77. Throw some nuts to (them / those) squirrels.

78. I'm studying (for / so) I can graduate.

79. I'm running to the market (for / because) we're out of milk.

80. People should live their own (lifes / lives).

81. (It's / Its) just too hot.

82. Do you (have / got) any catsup?

83. I will (tell / ask) her where she was when I called.

84. She doesn't have (anything / nothing) more to say.

85. I won't take my jacket (cause / because) it's hot outside.

86. We're going (to / too)!

87. That was a big (lost / loss) for our football team.

88. I'll brush my teeth and (than / then) we'll leave.

89. How many members (are / our) here today?

90. (Were / We're) we all there at the same time?

91. I (suppose / supposed) it's okay. Ask your dad.

92. Please (accept / except) my thanks for your help.

93. Are you going (everywhere / anywhere), or staying home?

94. There's the dog. Where's (it's / its) owner?

95. He's coming (at / until) 4:30.

96. Let's go (when / went) he gets here.

97. I (though / thought) I already did that!

98. Let's go (threw / through) the song one more time.

99. (Are / Our) team is great this year.

100. The airport is over (there/ their / they're).

101. (Whose / Who's) scarf is this?

102. She will come back (on / until) Tuesday.

103. It's time to (close / turn off) the radio.

104. They (when / went) to the laundromat.

105. (You're / Your) cute!

106. My sunburn is (worse / worst) than yours.

107. This road is the (worse / worst) in all 50 states.

108. The mall is (too / very) close. We can walk to it.

109. I (stood / stayed) at my aunt's last night.

110. He said he will (pass by / come to) the party.

111. I (fell / feel) sorry for him.

112. There aren't (any / no) trees in this park!

113. (May be / Maybe) I can go.

114. I'm going to bed (cause / because) I'm tired.

115. They have to (go walking / walk) to school.

116. He has really (tall / long) legs.

117. Her secretary (stepped out / left) for the day.

118. Do you want some ice cream? (I'd like that. / I don't mind.)

119. This test is over (right now)!

Text • Answer Key

Accept and Except

Story
1. except
2. accept
3. except
4. accept
5. accept
6. except

Practice
1. accept
2. accept
3. except
4. except
5. accept
6. accept
7. except
8. accept
9. except
10. except
11. accept

Ain't

Story
1. don't have
2. doesn't have
3. aren't
4. am not
5. isn't
6. haven't
7. am not

Practice
1. am not
2. isn't
3. aren't
4. aren't
5. isn't
6. don't have
7. isn't
8. doesn't have
9. don't have, doesn't have
10. aren't, am not
11. Isn't

Anywhere and Everywhere

Story
1. everywhere
2. Anywhere
3. everywhere
4. anywhere
5. anywhere

Practice
1. Everywhere
2. anywhere
3. anywhere
4. everywhere
5. anywhere

6. everywhere
7. anywhere
8. everywhere
9. anywhere
10. everywhere

Ask and Tell

Story
1. tell
2. tell
3. tell
4. ask
5. tell
6. Ask

Practice
1. ask
2. ask
3. ask
4. tell
5. Ask
6. ask
7. Tell
8. ask
9. ask
10. tell
11. ask

Barely and Just

Story
1. just
2. barely
3. just
4. just
5. barely

Practice
1. just
2. just
3. barely
4. just
5. barely
6. just
7. barely
8. barely
9. just
10. barely
11. barely
12. just

Borrow and Loan

Story
1. loan
2. loan
3. borrow
4. borrow
5. loan
6. loan
7. borrow

Practice
1. borrow
2. loan
3. borrow
4. borrow
5. loan
6. loan
7. borrow
8. loan
9. borrow
10. loan

Brake and Break

Story
1. break
2. break
3. break
4. brake
5. brake
6. break

Practice
1. brake
2. Break
3. break
4. break
5. break
6. break
7. brake
8. break
9. Break
10. brake
11. break
12. break

Can and May

Story
1. can
2. can
3. may
4. can
5. may
6. can
7. may

Practice
1. May
2. May
3. Can
4. may
5. can
6. May
7. can
8. can
9. can
10. may
11. May

Cause and Because

Story
1. because
2. cause
3. because
4. cause
5. cause
6. because

Practice
1. cause
2. Because
3. because
4. cause
5. because
6. cause
7. cause
8. because
9. cause
10. cause
11. cause
12. because

Close and Turn/Shut Off

Story
1. close
2. turn off/shut off
3. turn off/shut off
4. turn off/shut off
5. close

Practice
1. turn off/shut off
2. turn off/shut off
3. Close
4. close
5. turn off/shut off
6. turn off/shut off
7. turn off/shut off
8. turn off/shut off
9. turn off/shut off
10. turn off/shut off
11. close
12. turn off/shut off

Doesn't with No and Any

Story
1. no
2. no
3. any
4. any

Practice
1. any
2. any
3. no
4. any
5. any

6. no
7. any
8. any
9. any
10. any
11. no
12. any

Doesn't with None and Any

Story
1. none
2. none
3. any
4. any
5. any

Practice
1. any
2. any
3. any
4. none
5. none
6. none
7. any
8. any
9. none
10. any
11. any
12. any

Doesn't with Nothing and Anything

Story
1. nothing
2. anything
3. anything
4. anything
5. nothing

Practice
1. nothing
2. anything
3. anything
4. nothing
5. anything
6. anything
7. anything
8. anything
9. anything
10. anything
11. anything
12. nothing

Don't and Doesn't

Story
1. doesn't
2. doesn't
3. doesn't
4. doesn't
5. don't
6. doesn't
7. doesn't
8. doesn't
9. doesn't
10. doesn't

Practice
1. doesn't
2. don't
3. doesn't
4. Doesn't
5. doesn't
6. doesn't
7. doesn't
8. don't
9. doesn't
10. doesn't
11. doesn't
12. Don't

Don't Have To

Story
1. not supposed to/not allowed to
2. not supposed to/not allowed to
3. must not
4. must not

Practice
1. don't have to
2. must not
3. don't have to
4. must not
5. not supposed to/not allowed to
6. must not
7. not allowed to
8. not supposed to/not allowed to
9. must not

Don't with No and Any

Story
1. any
2. no
3. any
4. no
5. any

Practice
1. no
2. any
3. any
4. any
5. any
6. no
7. any
8. any
9. any
10. no
11. any

Don't with None and Any

Story
1. any
2. any
3. None
4. None

Practice
1. none
2. any
3. any
4. none
5. any
6. any
7. any
8. any
9. any
10. any
11. any

Don't with Nothing and Anything

Story
1. Nothing
2. anything
3. anything
4. anything
5. nothing

Practice
1. nothing
2. anything
3. anything
4. nothing
5. anything
6. anything
7. anything
8. nothing
9. anything
10. anything
11. anything

Either and Neither

Story
1. Either
2. neither
3. Neither
4. either
5. either

Practice
1. either
2. Neither
3. Neither
4. neither
5. either
6. either
7. Neither
8. either
9. either
10. either
11. neither

Else and More

Story
1. more
2. else
3. more
4. more
5. else

Practice
1. more
2. else
3. else
4. more
5. else
6. more
7. more
8. more
9. else
10. else
11. else
12. else

Every Time and All the Time

Story
1. Every time
2. all the time
3. every time
4. every time
5. all the time
6. all the time
7. all the time

Practice
1. Every time
2. all the time
3. Every time
4. every time
5. Every time

6. all the time
7. all the time
8. Every time
9. all the time
10. every time
11. Every time

Feel and Fell

Story
1. fell
2. feel
3. feel
4. fell
5. feel

Practice
1. feel
2. feel
3. fell
4. fell
5. fell
6. feel
7. feel
8. feel
9. feel
10. fell
11. fell
12. feel

For and Because

Story
1. for
2. because
3. because
4. because
5. for

Practice
1. because
2. because
3. because
4. because
5. for
6. because
7. because
8. because
9. for
10. because
11. because

For and So

Story
1. so
2. so
3. so
4. for
5. so

Practice
1. so

2. for
3. so
4. for
5. so
6. so
7. so
8. so
9. so
10. so
11. for
12. so

Go Walking and Walk

Story
1. walk
2. walk
3. go walking

Practice
1. walk
2. go walking
3. walk
4. go walking/walk
5. walk
6. walk
7. walk
8. walk
9. walk
10. walk

Gonna

Story
1. going to
2. going to
3. going to
4. going to
5. going to
6. going to
7. going to
8. going to
9. going to
10. not going to

Practice
1. going to/not going to
2. not going to
3. going to/not going to
4. going to
5. not going to
6. going to
7. not going to
8. going to/not going to
9. going to/not going to
10. going to
11. going to/not going to
12. going to

Got and Have

Story
1. have
2. have
3. have
4. got
5. have

Practice
1. have
2. have
3. got
4. have
5. have
6. have
7. got
8. have
9. have
10. have
11. have
12. got

Have and Of

Story
1. would have
2. could have
3. should have
4. of
5. might have

Practice
1. of
2. have
3. have
4. have
5. have
6. of
7. have
8. have
9. have
10. have
11. have
12. have

He's and His

Story
1. He's
2. His
3. he's
4. his
5. His
6. he's
7. he's

Practice
1. his
2. his
3. his

4. His
5. he's, his
6. He's
7. He's
8. his
9. his
10. He's
11. His
12. He's, his

I Don't Mind

Story
1. I'd like that
2. I don't mind
3. I don't mind

Practice
1. I'd like that
2. I'd like that
3. I don't mind
4. I don't mind
5. I'd like that

Its and It's

Story
1. It's
2. its
3. it's
4. its
5. Its
6. it's

Practice
1. It's
2. it's
3. its
4. It's
5. its
6. it's
7. its
8. its
9. It's, its
10. its
11. It's
12. It's

Just and Right Now

Story
1. just
2. right now
3. just
4. right now
5. right now

Practice
1. right now
2. just
3. right now

4. just
5. just
6. right now
7. right now
8. just
9. just
10. right now
11. right now
12. just

Left To

Story
1. left to
2. left for/left to go to
3. left for/left to go to

Practice
1. left for/left to go to
2. left for/left to go to
3. left to
4. left for/left to go to
5. left for/left to go to
6. left to go to/left to
7. left for/left to go to
8. left for/left to go to
9. left to go to/left to
10. left for/left to go to
11. left for

Less and Fewer

Story
1. less
2. fewer
3. less
4. fewer
5. less

Practice
1. less
2. fewer
3. fewer
4. less
5. fewer
6. less
7. fewer
8. fewer
9. Less
10. less, fewer
11. fewer
12. less

Life and Lives

Story
1. Life
2. life

3. lives
4. lives
5. life
6. lives
7. life

Practice
1. life
2. lives
3. lives
4. lives
5. lives
6. lives
7. life
8. lives
9. wolves
10. shelves
11. knives
12. calves
13. lives

Long and Tall

Story
1. tall
2. long
3. tall
4. tall
5. long

Practice
1. long
2. long
3. long
4. tall
5. long
6. tall
7. long
8. tall
9. long
10. tall
11. tall

Lose and Loose

Story
1. lose
2. loose
3. lose
4. loose
5. lose

Practice
1. lose
2. lose
3. loose
4. loose
5. lose
6. loose

7. loose
8. loose
9. lose
10. lose
11. lose
12. loose

Loss and Lost

Story
1. lost
2. loss
3. lost
4. loss
5 lost

Practice
1. lost
2. lost
3. Lost
4. lost
5. lost, loss
6. loss
7. lost
8. loss
9. lost
10. lost
11. loss

Make and Give a Party

Story
1. give/throw/have
2. make
3. make
4. give/throw/have
5. give/throw/have
6. give/throw/have
7. make

Practice
1. give/throw/have
2. make
3. give/throw/have
4. give/throw/have
5. give/throw/have
6. give/throw/have
7. give/throw/have
8. give/throw/have
9. make
10. give/throw/have

Married With and To

Story
1. to
2. to
3. with
4. to

Practice
1. to
2. with
3. to
4. with
5. to
6. to
7. with
8. to
9. to
10. to

Might Can, and Maybe

Story
1. may be able to
2. Maybe
3. may be able to
4. may be able to
5. maybe

Practice
1. may be able to
2. may be able to
3. may be able to
4. may be able to
5. Maybe
6. Maybe
7. Maybe
8. may be able to
9. may be able to
10. Maybe
11. Maybe, maybe

Mines and Mine

Story
1. mines
2. mines
3. mines
4. mine
5. mine
6. mine
7. mine

Practice
1. mines
2. mines
3. mines
4. mine
5. mine
6. mine
7. mines
8. mine
9. mine
10. Mine

No and Know

Story
1. no
2. know
3. no
4. know
5. know
6. know
7. no
8. no
9. no

Practice
1. know, no
2. no
3. know
4. No
5. know
6. know
7. no
8. know
9. know
10. know
11. know
12. know

Not with Nothing and Anything

Story
1. anything
2. anything
3. anything
4. anything
5. nothing

Practice
1. anything
2. anything
3. nothing
4. anything
5. anything
6. anything
7. nothing
8. anything
9. anything
10. anything
11. nothing

Now and Know

Story
1. now
2. know
3. know
4. Now
5. know
6. now
7. know

8. now
9. now

Practice
1. know, now
2. Know, Now
3. Now, know
4. know, know
5. know
6. know
7. know
8. now
9. know
10. now
11. know
12. know

Our and Are

Story
1. are
2. our
3. are
4. our
5. Are
6. are
7. our
8. are
9. are
10. our
11. our
12. Are
13. Are

Practice
1. are, our
2. are, our
3. Are
4. our, are
5. Our, are
6. Are, our
7. Our, our
8. Are, are
9. are
10. Our, are
11. Our
12. are

Pass By and Stop By

Story
1. come over
2. show up
3. pass by
4. stop by

Practice
1. Come over
2. show up
3. come over

4. come over/show up/stop by
5. pass by
6. come over/show up/stop by
7. pass by
8. pass by
9. come over/show up/stop by
10. come over/show up/stop by
11. come over/show up/stop by

Past and Passed

Story
1. past
2. passed
3. passed
4. passed
5. passed
6. past

Practice
1. passed
2. passed
3. passed
4. past
5. past
6. past
7. passed
8. past
9. past
10. passed
11. passed

Right Now and Already

Story
1. right now
2. already
3. already
4. right now
5. Right now

Practice
1. already
2. right now
3. right now
4. already
5. already
6. right now
7. already
8. already
9. already
10. right now

Sense and Since

Story
1. since
2. sense
3. sense
4. since

5. sense

Practice
1. sense
2. sense
3. since
4. sense
5. sense
6. Since
7. since
8. since
9. Since
10. sense
11. sense
12. since

Stayed and Stood

Story
1. stood
2. stayed
3. stood
4. stayed

Practice
1. stayed
2. stood
3. stood
4. stayed
5. stayed
6. stood
7. stayed
8. stayed
9. stayed
10. stood
11. stood
12. stayed

Stepped Out and Left

Story
1. left
2. stepped out
3. isn't in

Practice
1. stepped out
2. left
3. left/isn't in
4. isn't in
5. left/isn't in
6. stepped
7. left
8. left
9. left
10. isn't in

Suppose and Supposed To

Story
1. supposed to

2. suppose
3. supposed to
4. suppose
5. supposed to
6. suppose

Practice
1. suppose
2. suppose
3. supposed to
4. supposed to
5. Suppose
6. suppose
7. supposed to
8. suppposed to
9. supposed to
10. supposed to
11. suppose

Their, There, and They're

Story
1. their
2. they're
3. there
4. they're
5. their
6. there

Practice
1. their
2. They're
3. there
4. Their
5. their
6. They're, their
7. There
8. Their
9. There
10. They're

Them and Those

Story
1. them
2. Those
3. those
4. them
5. those

Practice
1. Those
2. them
3. those, those
4. those
5. those
6. them
7. those
8. Those
9. them

10. Those
11. those
12. those

Then and Than

Story
1. than
2. Then
3. than
4. Then
5. Then
6. than

Practice
1. Then
2. than
3. than
4. Then
5. than
6. Then
7. than
8. than
9. than
10. then
11. than

Thought and Though

Story
1. though
2. thought
3. though
4. thought
5. thought
6. thought

Practice
1. thought
2. thought
3. thought
4. thought
5. though
6. though
7. thought
8. though
9. though
10. thought, thought

Threw and Through

Story
1. through
2. threw
3. threw
4. through
5. through
6. through
7. through
8. through

Practice
1. through
2. threw, through
3. threw
4. through
5. through
6. through
7. threw
8. threw
9. threw
10. through
11. threw
12. through

To and Too (as in also)

Story
1. to
2. to
3. to
4. to
5. too
6. to
7. too

Practice
1. too
2. to
3. to
4. too
5. too
6. to, to
7. too
8. to
9. too
10. too
11. too
12. too

To and Too (as in bad)

Story
1. to
2. to
3. to
4. too
5. to
6. too
7. too
8. too
9. too
10. to
11. to
12. too
13. to
14. to

Practice
1. too, to
2. too, to

3. Too
4. too
5. too, to
6. to, too, to
7. to, too
8. to
9. too
10. too
11. too
12. too

Too and Very

Story
1. very
2. too
3. too
4. very
5. very
6. too
7. very

Practice
1. too
2. very
3. too
4. very
5. too
6. too
7. very
8. too
9. very
10. too
11. very
12. too

Until

Story
1. can't/won't
2. can't/won't
3. can't/won't
4. not

Practice
1. not
2. can't/won't
3. won't
4. can't/won't
5. won't
6. can't/won't
7. not
8. can't/won't
9. not
10. not
11. can't/won't
12. won't

Text • Answer Key

Vacations and Vacation

Story
1. vacation
2. vacation
3. vacations
4. vacations
5. vacation

Practice
1. vacation
2. vacation
3. vacation
4. vacations
5. vacation
6. vacation
7. vacation
8. vacation
9. vacation

We're and Were

Story
1. We're
2. were
3. were
4. we're
5. we're
6. we're
7. We're
8. We're

Practice
1. Were
2. We're
3. we're
4. Were
5. we're
6. we're
7. We're
8. were
9. We're, were
10. We're
11. were

When and Went

Story
1. When
2. went
3. when
4. When
5. went
6. when
7. When

Practice
1. When
2. when
3. went, when
4. when

5. went
6. went
7. when
8. when
9. went
10. when
11. went, when
12. When, went

Whether and Weather

Story
1. whether
2. whether
3. whether
4. weather

Practice
1. weather
2. whether
3. whether
4. weather
5. Whether
6. whether
7. whether
8. weather
9. weather
10. weather
11. weather

Who's and Whose

Story
1. Who's
2. Whose
3. Who's
4. Whose
5. Whose
6. who's

Practice
1. Who's
2. whose
3. whose
4. Whose
5. Who's
6. whose
7. Who's
8. who's
9. Who's
10. whose
11. Whose

Worse and Worst

Story
1. worse
2. worst
3. worse

4. worst
5. worse

Practice
1. worse
2. worst
3. worse
4. worst
5. worse
6. worse
7. worse
8. worst
9. worst
10. worst
11. worst

You're and Your Practice

Story
1. You're
2. your
3. You're
4. your
5. your
6. you're

Practice
1. your
2. you're
3. You're
4. your
5. You're
6. your
7. you're
8. You're
9. your
10. You're
11. Your

1. loose	41. any	81. It's
2. fewer	42. cause	82. have
3. He's	43. have	83. ask
4. going to	44. lives	84. anything
5. because	45. lose	85. because
6. else	46. supposed	86. too
7. any	47. their	87. loss
8. must not	48. past	88. then
9. turn off	49. too	89. are
10. break	50. know	90. Were
11. ask	51. anything	91. suppose
12. except	52. to	92. accept
13. loan	53. threw	93. anywhere
14. nothing	54. whether	94. its
15. lost	55. know	95. at
16. give	56. less	96. when
17. mine	57. for	97. thought
18. our	58. any	98. through
19. since	59. loan	99. Our
20. They're	60. just	100. there
21. we're	61. must not	101. Whose
22. worse	62. doesn't	102. on
23. thought	63. brake	103. turn off
24. passed	64. can	104. went
25. know	65. anything	105. You're
26. to	66. Neither	106. worse
27. any	67. have	107. worst
28. barely	68. Every time	108. very
29. anything	69. than	109. stayed
30. may	70. You're	110. come to
31. all the time	71. weather	111. feel
32. feel	72. vacation	112. any
33. so	73. When	113. Maybe
34. everywhere	74. now	114. because
35. those	75. your	115. walk
36. vacation	76. sense	116. long
37. any	77. those	117. left
38. doesn't	78. so	118. I'd like that
39. either	79. because	119. right now
40. else	80. lives	

Notes